Advance praise for *Daring Greatly*

"A wonderful book: urgent, essential, and fun to read. I couldn't put it down, and it continues to resonate with me."

—Seth Godin, *New York Times* bestselling author of *Linchpin*

"The brilliantly insightful Brené Brown draws upon extensive research and personal experience to explore the paradoxes of courage: We become strong by embracing vulnerability, we dare more greatly when we acknowledge our fear. I can't stop thinking about this book."

—Gretchen Rubin, *New York Times* bestselling author of
The Happiness Project and *Happiness at Home*

"In *Daring Greatly*, Brené Brown refers to herself as both a mapmaker and a traveler. In my book, that makes her a guide. And I believe the world needs more guides like her who are showing us a wiser way to our inner world. If you'd like to set your course on being more courageous and connected, engaged and resilient, leave the GPS at home. *Daring Greatly* is all the navigation you'll need."

—Maria Shriver, *New York Times* bestselling author of
Just Who Will You Be?

"*Daring Greatly* is an important book—a timely warning about the danger of pursuing certainty and control above all. Brené Brown offers all of us a valuable guide to the real reward of vulnerability: greater courage."

—Daniel H. Pink, *New York Times* bestselling author of
Drive and *A Whole New Mind*

"What I find remarkable about this book is the unique combination of solid research and kitchen-table storytelling. Brené becomes such a real person in the book that you can actually hear her voice asking, '*Have you dared greatly today?*' The invitation in this book is clear: We must be larger than anxiety, fear, and shame if we want to speak, act, and show up. The world needs this book and Brené's unique blend of warmth, humor, and butt-kicking makes her the perfect person to inspire us to dare greatly."

—Harriet Lerner, Ph.D., *New York Times* bestselling author of
The Dance of Anger and *Marriage Rules:*
A Manual for the Married and the Coupled Up

"One of the tragic ironies of modern life is that so many people feel isolated from each other by the very feelings they have in common: including a fear of failure and a sense of not being enough. Brené Brown shines a bright light into these dark recesses of human emotion and reveals how these feelings can gnaw at fulfillment in education, at work, and in the home. She shows too how they can be transformed to help us live more wholehearted lives of courage, engagement, and purpose. Brené Brown writes as she speaks, with wisdom, wit, candor, and a deep sense of humanity. If you're a student, teacher, parent, employer, employee, or just alive and wanting to live more fully, you should read this book. I double dare you."

—Sir Ken Robinson, *New York Times* bestselling author of
Out of Our Minds and The Element:
How Finding Your Passion Changes Everything

"Here's the essence of this book: Vulnerability is courage in you but inadequacy in me. Brené's book, weaving together research and Texan anecdote, shows you the path forward. And don't for a moment think this is only for women. Men carry the burden of *being strong and never weak*, and we pay a heavy price for it. *Daring Greatly* can help us all."

—Michael Bungay Stanier, author of *Do More Great Work*

"I deeply trust Brené Brown—her research, her intelligence, her integrity, and her personhood. So when she definitively lands on the one most important value we can cultivate for professional success, relationship health, parental joy, and courageous, passionate living . . . well, I sit up and take notice. And even when that one most critical value turns out to be the risky act of being *vulnerable*. Brené dared greatly to write this book, and you will benefit greatly to read it and to put its razor-sharp wisdom into action in your own life and work."

—Elizabeth Lesser, *New York Times* bestselling author of
Broken Open: How Difficult Times Can Help Us Grow
and cofounder of the Omega Institute

"In an age of constant pressure to conform and pretend, *Daring Greatly* offers a compelling alternative: Transform your life by being who you really are. Embrace the courage to be vulnerable. Dare to read this book!"

—Chris Guillebeau, *New York Times* bestselling author of *The $100 Startup*

DARING GREATLY

DARING GREATLY

How the
Courage to
Be Vulnerable
Transforms
the Way
We Live,
Love, Parent,
and Lead

BRENÉ BROWN, Ph.D., LMSW

GOTHAM
BOOKS

GOTHAM BOOKS
Published by Penguin Group (USA) Inc.
375 Hudson Street, New York, New York 10014, U.S.A.
Penguin Group (Canada), 90 Eglinton Avenue East, Suite 700, Toronto, Ontario
M4P 2Y3, Canada (a division of Pearson Penguin Canada Inc.); Penguin Books
Ltd, 80 Strand, London WC2R 0RL, England; Penguin Ireland, 25 St Stephen's
Green, Dublin 2, Ireland (a division of Penguin Books Ltd); Penguin Group
(Australia), 250 Camberwell Road, Camberwell, Victoria 3124, Australia (a divi-
sion of Pearson Australia Group Pty Ltd); Penguin Books India Pvt Ltd, 11 Com-
munity Centre, Panchsheel Park, New Delhi–110 017, India; Penguin Group
(NZ), 67 Apollo Drive, Rosedale, Auckland 0632, New Zealand (a division of
Pearson New Zealand Ltd); Penguin Books (South Africa) (Pty) Ltd, 24 Sturdee
Avenue, Rosebank, Johannesburg 2196, South Africa

Penguin Books Ltd, Registered Offices: 80 Strand, London WC2R 0RL, England

Published by Gotham Books, a member of Penguin Group (USA) Inc.

First printing, September 2012
20 19 18

LIBRARY OF CONGRESS CATALOGING-IN-PUBLICATION DATA
Brown, C. Brené.
    Daring greatly : how the courage to be vulnerable transforms the way we live,
love, parent, and lead / Brené Brown.—1st ed.
        p. cm.
    Includes bibliographical references.
    ISBN 978-1-592-40733-0
    1. Assertiveness (Psychology) 2. Risk. 3. Courage. I. Title.
    BF575.A85B76 2012
    158—dc23   2012018649

Printed in the United States of America
Set in Janson Text
Designed by Spring Hoteling

While the author has made every effort to provide accurate telephone numbers,
Internet addresses, and other contact information at the time of publication, neither the publisher nor the author assumes any responsibility for errors, or for
changes that occur after publication. Further, the publisher does not have any control over and does not assume any responsibility for author or third-party websites
or their content.

Except for friends and family, names and identifying characteristics of individuals
mentioned have been changed to protect their privacy.

To Steve
You make the world a better place
and me a braver person.

CONTENTS

WHAT IT MEANS TO DARE GREATLY

THE phrase *Daring Greatly* is from Theodore Roosevelt's speech "Citizenship in a Republic." The speech, sometimes referred to as "The Man in the Arena," was delivered at the Sorbonne in Paris, France, on April 23, 1910. This is the passage that made the speech famous:

> "It is not the critic who counts; not the man who points out how the strong man stumbles, or where the doer of deeds could have done them better.

> The credit belongs to the man who is actually in the arena, whose face is marred by dust and sweat and blood; who strives valiantly; who errs, who comes short again and again,

> because there is no effort without error and shortcoming; but who does actually strive to do the deeds; who knows great enthusiasms, the great devotions; who spends himself in a worthy cause;

> who at the best knows in the end the triumph of high achievement, and who at the worst, if he fails, at least fails while daring greatly. . . ."

The first time I read this quote, I thought, *This is vulnerability. Everything I've learned from over a decade of research on vulnerability has taught me this exact lesson. Vulnerability is not knowing victory or defeat, it's understanding the necessity of both; it's engaging. It's being all in.*

Vulnerability is not weakness, and the uncertainty, risk, and emotional exposure we face every day are not optional. Our only choice is a question of engagement. Our willingness to own and engage with our vulnerability determines the depth of our courage and the clarity of our purpose; the level to which we protect ourselves from being vulnerable is a measure of our fear and disconnection.

When we spend our lives waiting until we're perfect or bulletproof before we walk into the arena, we ultimately sacrifice relationships and opportunities that may not be recoverable, we squander our precious time, and we turn our backs on our gifts, those unique contributions that only we can make.

Perfect and *bulletproof* are seductive, but they don't exist in the human experience. We must walk into the arena, whatever it may be—a new relationship, an important meeting, our creative process, or a difficult family conversation—with courage and the willingness to engage. Rather than sitting on the sidelines and hurling judgment and advice, **we must dare to show up and let ourselves be seen**. This is vulnerability. This is *daring greatly*.

Join me as we explore the answers to these questions:

- What drives our fear of being vulnerable?
- How are we protecting ourselves from vulnerability?

- What price are we paying when we shut down and disengage?

- How do we own and engage with vulnerability so we can start transforming the way we live, love, parent, and lead?

INTRODUCTION: MY ADVENTURES IN THE ARENA

I looked right at her and said, "I frickin' hate vulnerability." I figured she's a therapist—I'm sure she's had tougher cases. Plus, the sooner she knows what she's dealing with, the faster we can get this whole therapy thing wrapped up. "I hate uncertainty. I hate not knowing. I can't stand opening myself to getting hurt or being disappointed. It's excruciating. Vulnerability is complicated. *And* it's excruciating. Do you know what I mean?"

Diana nods. "Yes, I know vulnerability. I know it well. It's an exquisite emotion." Then she looks up and kind of smiles, as if she's picturing something really beautiful. I'm sure I look confused because I can't imagine what she's picturing. I'm suddenly concerned for her well-being and my own.

"I said it was *excruciating*, not *exquisite*," I point out. "And let me say this for the record, if my research didn't link being vulnerable with living a Whole-hearted life, I wouldn't be here. I hate how it makes me feel."

"What does it feel like?"

"Like I'm coming out of my skin. Like I need to fix whatever's happening and make it better."

"And if you can't?"

"Then I feel like punching someone in the face."

"And do you?"

"No. Of course not."

"So what do you do?"

"Clean the house. Eat peanut butter. Blame people. Make everything around me perfect. Control whatever I can—whatever's not nailed down."

"When do you feel the most vulnerable?"

"When I'm in fear." I look up as Diana responds with that annoying pause and head-nodding done by therapists to draw us out. "When I'm anxious and unsure about how things are going to go, or if I'm having a difficult conversation, or if I'm trying something new or doing something that makes me uncomfortable or opens me up to criticism or judgment." Another annoying pause as the empathic nodding continues. "When I think about how much I love my kids and Steve, and how my life would be over if something happened to them. When I see the people I care about struggling, and I can't fix it or make it better. All I can do is be with them."

"I see."

"I feel it when I'm scared that things are too good. Or too scary. I'd really like for it to be exquisite, but right now it's just excruciating. Can people change that?"

"Yes, I believe they can."

"Can you give me some homework or something? Should I review the data?"

"No data and no homework. No assignments or gold stars in here. Less thinking. More feeling."

"Can I get to exquisite without having to feel really vulnerable in the process?"

"No."

"Well, shit. That's just awesome."

If you don't know anything about me from my other books, my blog, or the TED videos that have gone viral online, let me catch you up. If, on the other hand, you're already a little queasy from the mention of a therapist, skip this chapter entirely and go straight to the appendix about my research process. I have spent my entire life trying to outrun and outsmart vulnerability. I'm a fifth-generation Texan with a family motto of "lock and load," so I come by my aversion to uncertainty and emotional exposure honestly (and genetically). By middle school, which is the time when most of us begin to wrestle with vulnerability, I began to develop and hone my vulnerability-avoidance skills.

Over time I tried everything from "the good girl" with my "perform-perfect-please" routine, to clove-smoking poet, angry activist, corporate climber, and out-of-control party girl. At first glance these may seem like reasonable, if not predictable, developmental stages, but they were more than that for me. All of my stages were different suits of armor that kept me from becoming too engaged and too vulnerable. Each strategy was built on the same premise: *Keep everyone at a safe distance and always have an exit strategy.*

Along with my fear of vulnerability, I also inherited a huge heart and ready empathy. So, in my late twenties, I left a management position at AT&T, got a job waiting tables and bartending, and went back to school to become a social worker. When I met with my boss at AT&T to resign, I'll never forget her response: "Let me guess. You're leaving to become a social worker or an MTV VJ on *Headbanger's Ball*?"

Like many of the folks drawn to social work, I liked the idea of fixing people and systems. By the time I was done with my bachelor's degree (BSW) and was finishing my master's degree (MSW), though, I had realized that social work wasn't about fixing. It was and is all about contextualizing and "leaning in." Social work is all about leaning into the discomfort of ambiguity and uncertainty, and holding open an empathic space so people can find their own way. In a word—*messy*.

As I struggled to figure out how I could ever make a career in social work actually work, I was riveted by a statement from one of my research professors: "If you can't measure it, it doesn't exist." He explained that unlike our other classes in the program, research was all about prediction and control. I was smitten. You mean that rather than leaning and holding, I could spend my career predicting and controlling? I had found my calling.

The surest thing I took away from my BSW, MSW, and Ph.D. in social work is this: Connection is why we're here. We are hardwired to connect with others, it's what gives purpose and meaning to our lives, and without it there is suffering. I wanted to develop research that explained the anatomy of connection.

Studying connection was a simple idea, but before I knew it, I had been hijacked by my research participants who, when asked to talk about their most important relationships and experiences of connection, kept telling me about heartbreak, betrayal, and shame—the fear of not being worthy of real connection. We humans have a tendency to define things by what they are not. This is especially true of our emotional experiences.

By accident, then, I became a shame and empathy researcher, spending six years developing a theory that explains what shame is, how it works, and how we cultivate resilience in the face of believing that we're not enough—that we're not worthy of love and belonging. In 2006 I realized that in addition to understanding shame, I had to understand the flip side: "What do the people who are the most resilient to shame, who believe in their worthiness—I call these people the Wholehearted—have in common?"

I hoped like hell that the answer to this question would be: "They are shame researchers. To be Wholehearted, you have to know a lot about shame." But I was wrong. Understanding shame is only one variable that contributes to Wholeheartedness, a way of engaging with the world from a place of worthiness. In *The Gifts of Imperfection*, I defined ten "guideposts" for Wholehearted living that point to what the Wholehearted work to cultivate and what they work to let go of:

1. Cultivating Authenticity: Letting Go of What People Think
2. Cultivating Self-Compassion: Letting Go of Perfectionism
3. Cultivating a Resilient Spirit: Letting Go of Numbing and Powerlessness
4. Cultivating Gratitude and Joy: Letting Go of Scarcity and Fear of the Dark
5. Cultivating Intuition and Trusting Faith: Letting Go of the Need for Certainty
6. Cultivating Creativity: Letting Go of Comparison
7. Cultivating Play and Rest: Letting Go of Exhaustion as a Status Symbol and Productivity as Self-Worth
8. Cultivating Calm and Stillness: Letting Go of Anxiety as a Lifestyle
9. Cultivating Meaningful Work: Letting Go of Self-Doubt and "Supposed To"

10. Cultivating Laughter, Song, and Dance: Letting Go of Being Cool and "Always in Control"

As I analyzed the data, I realized that I was about two for ten in my own life when in comes to Wholehearted living. That was personally devastating. This happened a few weeks before my forty-first birthday and sparked my midlife unraveling. As it turns out, getting an intellectual handle on these issues isn't the same as living and loving with your whole heart.

I have written in great detail in *The Gifts of Imperfection* about what it means to be Wholehearted and about the ~~breakdown~~ spiritual awakening that ensued from this realization. But what I want to do here is to share the definition of Wholehearted living and share the five most important themes that emerged from the data and which led me to the breakthroughs I share in this book. It will give you an idea of what's ahead:

Wholehearted living is about engaging in our lives from a place of worthiness. It means cultivating the courage, compassion, and connection to wake up in the morning and think, *No matter what gets done and how much is left undone, I am enough.* It's going to bed at night thinking, *Yes, I am imperfect and vulnerable and sometimes afraid, but that doesn't change the truth that I am also brave and worthy of love and belonging.*

This definition is based on these fundamental ideals:

1. Love and belonging are irreducible needs of all men, women, and children. We're hardwired for connection—it's what gives purpose

and meaning to our lives. The absence of love, belonging, and connection always leads to suffering.

2. If you roughly divide the men and women I've interviewed into two groups—those who feel a deep sense of love and belonging, and those who struggle for it—there's only one variable that separates the groups: Those who feel lovable, who love, and who experience belonging simply believe they are *worthy* of love and belonging. They don't have better or easier lives, they don't have fewer struggles with addiction or depression, and they haven't survived fewer traumas or bankruptcies or divorces, but in the midst of all of these struggles, they have developed practices that enable them to hold on to the belief that they are worthy of love, belonging, and even joy.

3. A strong belief in our worthiness doesn't just happen—it's cultivated when we understand the guideposts as choices and daily practices.

4. The main concern of Wholehearted men and women is living a life defined by courage, compassion, and connection.

5. The Wholehearted identify vulnerability as the catalyst for courage, compassion, and connection. In fact, the willingness to be vulnerable emerged as the single clearest value shared by all of the women and men whom I would describe as Wholehearted. They attribute everything—from their professional success to

their marriages to their proudest parenting moments—to their ability to be vulnerable.

I had written about vulnerability in my earlier books; in fact, there's even a chapter on it in my dissertation. From the very beginning of my investigations, embracing vulnerability emerged as an important category. I also understood the relationships between vulnerability and the other emotions that I've studied. But in those previous books, I assumed that the relationships between vulnerability and different constructs like shame, belonging, and worthiness were coincidence. Only after twelve years of dropping deeper and deeper into this work did I finally understand the role it plays in our lives. Vulnerability is the core, the heart, the center, of meaningful human experiences.

This new information created a major dilemma for me personally: On the one hand, how can you talk about the importance of vulnerability in an honest and meaningful way without being vulnerable? On the other hand, how can you be vulnerable without sacrificing your legitimacy as a researcher? To be honest, I think emotional accessibility is a shame trigger for researchers and academics. Very early in our training, we are taught that a cool distance and inaccessibility contribute to prestige, and that if you're too relatable, your credentials come into question. While being called pedantic is an insult in most settings, in the ivory tower we're taught to wear the pedantic label like a suit of armor.

How could I risk being really vulnerable and tell stories about my own messy journey through this research without looking like a total flake? What about my professional armor?

My moment to "dare greatly," as Theodore Roosevelt once urged citizens to do, came in June 2010 when I was invited to speak at TEDxHouston. TEDxHouston is one of many independently organized events modeled after TED—a nonprofit addressing the worlds of Technology, Entertainment, and Design that is devoted to "Ideas Worth Spreading." TED and TEDx organizers bring together "the world's most fascinating thinkers and doers" and challenge them to give the talk of their life in eighteen minutes or less.

The TEDxHouston curators were unlike any event organizers I've known. Bringing in a shame-and-vulnerability researcher makes most organizers a little nervous and compels a few to get somewhat prescriptive about the content of the talk. When I asked the TEDx people what they wanted me to talk about, they responded, "We love your work. Talk about whatever makes you feel awesome—do your thing. We're grateful to share the day with you." Actually, I'm not sure how they made the decision to let me do my thing, because before that talk I wasn't aware of having *a thing*.

I loved the freedom of that invitation and I hated it. I was back straddling the tension between leaning into the discomfort and finding refuge in my old friends, prediction and control. I decided to go for it. *Truthfully, I had no idea what I was getting into.*

My decision to dare greatly didn't stem from self-confidence as much as it did from faith in my research. I know I'm a good researcher, and I trusted that the conclusions I had drawn from the data were valid and reliable. Vulnerability would take me where I wanted or maybe needed to go. I also convinced myself that it wasn't really a big deal: *It's Houston, a hometown crowd. Worst-case scenario, five hundred people plus a few watching the live streaming will think I'm a nut.*

The morning after the talk, I woke up with one of the worst vulnerability hangovers of my life. You know that feeling when you wake up and everything feels fine until the memory of laying yourself open washes over you and you want to hide under the covers? *What did I do? Five hundred people officially think I'm crazy and it totally sucks. I forgot to mention two important things. Did I actually have a slide with the word* breakdown *on it to reinforce the story that I shouldn't have told in the first place? I must leave town.*

But there was nowhere to run. Six months after the talk, I received an e-mail from the curators of TEDxHouston congratulating me because my talk was going to be featured on the main TED website. I knew that was a good thing, a coveted honor even, but I was terrified. First, I was just settling into the idea of "only" five hundred people thinking I'm crazy. Second, in a culture full of critics and cynics, I had always felt safer in my career flying right under the radar. Looking back, I'm not sure how I would have responded to that e-mail had I known that having a video go viral on vulnerability and the importance of letting ourselves be seen would leave me feeling so uncomfortably (and ironically) vulnerable and exposed.

Today that talk is one of the most viewed on TED.com, with more than five million hits and translation available in thirty-eight languages. I've never watched it. I'm glad I did it, but it still makes me feel really uncomfortable.

The way I see it, 2010 was the year of the TEDxHouston talk, and 2011 was the year of *walking the talk*—literally. I crisscrossed the country speaking to groups ranging from Fortune 500 companies, leadership coaches, and the military, to lawyers, parenting groups, and school districts. In 2012, I was invited to give another talk at the main TED conference in Long Beach, California. For me the 2012 talk was my opportunity to share the work that has literally been the foundation and springboard for all of my research—I talked about shame and how we have to understand it and work through it if we really want to dare greatly.

The experience of sharing my research led me to write this book. After discussions with my publisher about the possibility of a business book and/or a parenting book, plus a book for teachers, I realized that there only needed to be one book because no matter where I went or with whom I was speaking, the core issues were the same: fear, disengagement, and yearning for more courage.

My corporate talks almost always focus on inspired leadership or creativity and innovation. The most significant problems that everyone from C-level executives to the frontline folks talk to me about stem from disengagement, the lack of feedback, the fear of staying relevant amid rapid change, and the need for clarity of purpose. If we want to reignite innovation and passion, we have to rehumanize work. When shame becomes a management style, engagement dies. When failure is not an option we can forget about learning, creativity, and innovation.

When it comes to parenting, the practice of framing mothers and fathers as good or bad is both rampant and corrosive—it turns parenting into a shame minefield. The real questions for parents should be: "Are you engaged? Are you paying attention?" If so, plan to make lots of mistakes and bad decisions. Imperfect parenting moments turn into gifts as our children watch us try to figure out what went wrong and how we can do better next time. The mandate is not to be perfect and raise happy children. Perfection doesn't exist, and I've found that what makes children happy doesn't always prepare them to be courageous, engaged adults. The same is true for schools. I haven't encountered a single problem that isn't attributed to some combination of parental, teacher, administrative, and/or student disengagement and the clash of competing stakeholders vying to define one purpose.

I have found that the most difficult and most rewarding challenge of my work is how to be both a mapmaker and a traveler. My maps, or theories, on shame resilience, Wholeheartedness, and vulnerability have not been drawn from the experiences of my own travels, but from the data I've collected over the past dozen years—the experiences of thousands of men and women who are forging paths in the direction that I, and many others, want to take our lives.

Over the years I've learned that a surefooted and confident mapmaker does not a swift traveler make. I stumble and fall, and I constantly find myself needing to change course. And even though I'm trying to follow a map that I've drawn, there are many times when frustration and self-doubt take over, and I wad up that map and shove it into the junk drawer in my kitchen. It's not an easy journey from excruciating to exquisite, but for me it's been worth every step.

What we all share in common—what I've spent the past several years talking to leaders, parents, and educators about—is the truth that forms the very core of this book: *What we know matters, but who we are matters more.* Being rather than knowing requires showing up and letting ourselves be seen. It requires us to dare greatly, to be vulnerable. The first step of that journey is understanding where we are, what we're up against, and where we need to go. I think we can best do that by examining our pervasive "Never Enough" culture.

CHAPTER 1
SCARCITY:
LOOKING INSIDE OUR CULTURE OF "NEVER ENOUGH"

After doing this work for the past twelve years and watching scarcity ride roughshod over our families, organizations, and communities, I'd say the one thing we have in common is that we're sick of feeling afraid. We want to dare greatly. We're tired of the national conversation centering on "What should we fear?" and "Who should we blame?" We all want to be brave.

YOU can't swing a cat without hitting a narcissist."

Granted, it wasn't my most eloquent moment onstage. It also wasn't my intention to offend anyone, but when I'm really fired up or frustrated, I tend to revert back to the language instilled in me by the generations of Texans who came before me. I swing cats, things get stuck in my craw, and I'm frequently "fixin' to come undone." These regressions normally happen at home or when I'm with family and friends, but occasionally, when I'm feeling ornery, they slip out onstage.

I've heard and used the swinging-cat expression my entire life, and it didn't dawn on me that more than a few of the thousand members of the audience were picturing me knocking over self-important folks with an actual feline. In my defense, while responding to numerous e-mails sent by audience members who thought animal cruelty was inconsistent with my message of vulnerability and connection, I did learn that the expression has nothing to do with animals. It's actually a British Navy reference to the difficulty of using a cat-o'-nine-tails in the tight quarters of a ship. I know. Not so great either.

In this particular instance, the cat-swinging was

triggered when a woman from the audience shouted out, "The kids today think they're so special. What's turning so many people into narcissists?" My less-than-stellar response verged on smart-alecky: "Yeah. You can't swing a cat without hitting a narcissist." But it stemmed from a frustration that I still feel when I hear the term *narcissism* thrown around. *Facebook is so narcissistic. Why do people think what they're doing is so important? The kids today are all narcissists. It's always me, me, me. My boss is such a narcissist. She thinks she's better than everyone and is always putting other people down.*

And while laypeople are using narcissism as a catchall diagnosis for everything from arrogance to rude behavior, researchers and helping professionals are testing the concept's elasticity in every way imaginable. Recently a group of researchers conducted a computer analysis of three decades of hit songs. The researchers reported a statistically significant trend toward narcissism and hostility in popular music. In line with their hypothesis, they found a decrease in usages such as *we* and *us* and an increase in *I* and *me*.

The researchers also reported a decline in words related to social connection and positive emotions, and an increase in words related to anger and antisocial behavior, such as *hate* or *kill*. Two of the researchers from that study, Jean Twenge and Keith Campbell, authors of the book *The Narcissism Epidemic*, argue that the incidence of narcissistic personality disorder has more than doubled in the United States in the last ten years.

Relying on yet another fine saying from my grandmother, it feels like the world is going to hell in a handbasket.

Or is it? Are we surrounded by narcissists? Have we turned into a culture of self-absorbed, grandiose people who are only interested in power, success, beauty, and being special? Are we so entitled that we actually believe that we're superior even when we're not really contributing or achieving anything of value? Is it true that we lack the necessary empathy to be compassionate, connected people?

If you're like me, you're probably wincing a bit and thinking, *Yes. This is exactly the problem. Not with me, of course. But in general . . . this sounds about right!*

It feels good to have an explanation, especially one that conveniently makes us feel better about ourselves and places the blame on *those people*. In fact, whenever I hear people making the narcissism argument, it's normally served with a side of contempt, anger, and judgment. I'll be honest, I even felt those emotions when I was writing that paragraph.

Our first inclination is to cure "the narcissists" by cutting them down to size. It doesn't matter if I'm talking to teachers, parents, CEOs, or my neighbors, the response is the same: *These egomaniacs need to know that they're not special, they're not that great, they're not entitled to jack, and they need to get over themselves. No one cares.* (This is the G-rated version.)

Here's where it gets tricky. And frustrating. And maybe even a little heartbreaking. The topic of narcissism has penetrated the social consciousness enough that most people correctly associate it with a pattern of behaviors that include grandiosity, a pervasive need for admiration, and a lack of empathy. What almost no one understands is how every level of severity in this diagnosis is underpinned by shame. Which means we don't "fix it" by cutting people down to size and reminding folks of their inadequacies and smallness. Shame is more likely to be the cause of these behaviors, not the cure.

LOOKING AT NARCISSISM THROUGH
THE LENS OF VULNERABILITY

Diagnosing and labeling people whose struggles are more environmental or learned than genetic or organic is often far more detrimental to healing and change than it is helpful. And when we have an epidemic on our hands, unless we're talking about something physically contagious, the cause is much more likely to be environmental than a hardwiring issue. Labeling the problem in a way that makes it about who people are rather than the choices they're making lets all of us off the hook: *Too bad. That's who I am.* I'm a huge believer in holding people accountable for their behaviors, so I'm not talking about "blaming the system" here. I'm talking about understanding the root cause so we can address the problems.

It's often helpful to recognize patterns of behaviors and to understand what those patterns may indicate, but that's far different from becoming defined by a diagnosis, which is something I believe, and that the research shows, often exacerbates shame and prevents people from seeking help.

We need to understand these trends and influences, but I find it far more helpful, and even transformative in many instances, to look at the patterns of behaviors through the lens of vulnerability. For example, when I look at narcissism through the vulnerability lens, I **see the shame-based fear of being ordinary**. I see the fear of never feeling extraordinary enough to be noticed, to be lovable, to belong, or to cultivate a sense of purpose. Sometimes the simple act of humanizing problems sheds an important light on them, a light that often goes out the minute a stigmatizing label is applied.

This new definition of narcissism offers clarity and it illuminates both the source of the problem and possible solutions. I can see exactly how and why more people are wrestling with how to believe they are enough. I see the cultural messaging everywhere that says that an ordinary life is a meaningless life. And I see how kids that grow up on a steady diet of reality television, celebrity culture, and unsupervised social media can absorb this messaging and develop a completely skewed sense of the world. *I am only as good as the number of "likes" I get on Facebook or Instagram.*

Because we are all vulnerable to the messaging that drives these behaviors, this new lens takes away the us-versus-those-damn-narcissists element. I know the yearning to believe that what I'm doing matters and how easy it is to confuse that with the drive to be extraordinary. I know how seductive it is to use the celebrity culture yardstick to measure the smallness of our lives. And I also understand how grandiosity, entitlement, and admiration-seeking feel like just the right balm to soothe the ache of being too ordinary and inadequate. Yes, these thoughts and behaviors ultimately cause more pain and lead to more disconnection, but when we're hurting and when love and belonging are hanging in the balance, we reach for what we think will offer us the most protection.

There are certainly instances when a diagnosis might be necessary if we are to find the right treatment, but I can't think of one example where we don't benefit by also examining the struggle through the lens of vulnerability. Something can always be learned when we consider these questions:

1. What are the messages and expectations that define our culture and how does culture influence our behaviors?
2. How are our struggles and behaviors related to protecting ourselves?

3. How are our behaviors, thoughts, and emotions related to vulnerability and the need for
   a strong sense of worthiness?

If we go back to the earlier question of whether or not
we're surrounded by people with narcissistic personality disorder, my answer is no. There is a powerful cultural influence at play right now, and I think the fear of being ordinary
is a part of it, but I also think it goes deeper than that. To
find the source, we have to pan out past the name-calling and
labeling.

We've had the vulnerability lens zoomed in here on a few
specific behaviors, but if we pull out as wide as we can, the
view changes. We don't lose sight of the problems we've been
discussing, but we see them as part of a larger landscape. This
allows us to accurately identify the greatest cultural influence
of our time—the environment that not only explains what
everyone is calling a narcissism epidemic, but also provides a
panoramic view of the thoughts, behaviors, and emotions that
are slowly changing who we are and how we live, love, work,
lead, parent, govern, teach, and connect with one another.
This environment I'm talking about is our culture of scarcity.

SCARCITY: THE NEVER-ENOUGH PROBLEM

A critical aspect of my work is finding language that accurately represents the data *and* deeply resonates with participants. I know I'm off when people look as if they're pretending
to get it, or if they respond to my terms and definitions with
"huh" or "sounds interesting." Given the topics I study, I
know that I'm onto something when folks look away, quickly
cover their faces with their hands, or respond with "ouch,"
"shut up," or "get out of my head." The last is normally how

people respond when they hear or see the phrase: *Never* _____ *enough*. It only takes a few seconds before people fill in the blanks with their own tapes:

- Never good enough
- Never perfect enough
- Never thin enough
- Never powerful enough
- Never successful enough
- Never smart enough
- Never certain enough
- Never safe enough
- Never extraordinary enough

We get scarcity because we live it.

One of my very favorite writers on scarcity is global activist and fund-raiser Lynne Twist. In her book *The Soul of Money*, she refers to scarcity as "the great lie." She writes:

> For me, and for many of us, our first waking thought of the day is "I didn't get enough sleep." The next one is "I don't have enough time." Whether true or not, that thought of *not enough* occurs to us automatically before we even think to question or examine it. We spend most of the hours and the days of our lives hearing, explaining, complaining, or worrying about what we don't have enough

of. . . . Before we even sit up in bed, before our
feet touch the floor, we're already inadequate,
already behind, already losing, already lacking
something. And by the time we go to bed at
night, our minds are racing with a litany of
what we didn't get, or didn't get done, that day.
We go to sleep burdened by those thoughts
and wake up to that reverie of lack. . . . This
internal condition of scarcity, this mind-set of
scarcity, lives at the very heart of our jealou-
sies, our greed, our prejudice, and our arguments with life. . . . (43–45).

Scarcity is the "never enough" problem. The word *scarce*
is from the Old Norman French *scars*, meaning "restricted in
quantity" (c. 1300). Scarcity thrives in a culture where everyone is hyperaware of lack. Everything from safety and love to
money and resources feels restricted or lacking. We spend
inordinate amounts of time calculating how much we have,
want, and don't have, and how much everyone else has, needs,
and wants.

What makes this constant assessing and comparing so
self-defeating is that we are often comparing our lives, our
marriages, our families, and our communities to unattainable, media-driven visions of perfection, or we're holding up
our reality against our own fictional account of how great
someone else has it. Nostalgia is also a dangerous form of
comparison. Think about how often we compare ourselves
and our lives to a memory that nostalgia has so completely
edited that it never really existed: "Remember when . . . ?
Those were the days . . ."

THE SOURCE OF SCARCITY

Scarcity doesn't take hold in a culture overnight. But the feeling of scarcity does thrive in shame-prone cultures that are deeply steeped in comparison and fractured by disengagement. (By a shame-prone culture, I don't mean that we're ashamed of our collective identity, but that there are enough of us struggling with the issue of worthiness that it's shaping the culture.)

Over the past decade, I've witnessed major shifts in the zeitgeist of our country. I've seen it in the data, and honestly, I've seen it in the faces of the people I meet, interview, and talk to. The world has never been an easy place, but the past decade has been traumatic for so many people that it's made changes in our culture. From 9/11, multiple wars, and the recession, to catastrophic natural disasters and the increase in random violence and school shootings, we've survived and are surviving events that have torn at our sense of safety with such force that we've experienced them as trauma even if we weren't directly involved. And when it comes to the staggering numbers of those now unemployed and underemployed, I think every single one of us has been directly affected or is close to someone who has been directly affected.

Worrying about scarcity is our culture's version of post-traumatic stress. It happens when we've been through too much, and rather than coming together to heal (which requires vulnerability), we're angry and scared and at each other's throats. It's not just the larger culture that's suffering: I found the same dynamics playing out in family culture, work culture, school culture, and community culture. And they all share the same formula of shame, comparison, and disengagement. Scarcity bubbles up from these conditions and perpetuates them until a critical mass of people start making different choices and reshaping the smaller cultures they belong to.

One way to think about the three components of scarcity and how they influence culture is to reflect upon the following questions. As you're reading the questions, it's helpful to keep in mind any culture or social system that you're a part of, whether your classroom, your family, your community, or maybe your work team:

1. **Shame:** Is fear of ridicule and belittling used to manage people and/or to keep people in line? Is self-worth tied to achievement, productivity, or compliance? Are blaming and finger-pointing norms? Are put-downs and name-calling rampant? What about favoritism? Is perfectionism an issue?

2. **Comparison:** Healthy competition can be beneficial, but is there constant overt or covert comparing and ranking? Has creativity been suffocated? Are people held to one narrow standard rather than acknowledged for their unique gifts and contributions? Is there an ideal way of being or one form of talent that is used as measurement of everyone else's worth?

3. **Disengagement:** Are people afraid to take risks or try new things? Is it easier to stay quiet than to share stories, experiences, and ideas? Does it feel as if no one is really paying attention or listening? Is everyone struggling to be seen and heard?

When I look at these questions and think about our larger culture, the media, and the social-economic-political landscape, my answers are YES, YES, and YES!

When I think about my family in the context of these questions, I know that these are the exact issues that my husband, Steve, and I work to overcome every single day. I use the word *overcome* because to grow a relationship or raise a family or create an organizational culture or run a school or nurture a faith community, all in a way that is fundamentally opposite to the cultural norms driven by scarcity, it takes awareness, commitment, and work . . . every single day. The larger culture is always applying pressure, and unless we're willing to push back and fight for what we believe in, the default becomes a state of scarcity. We're called to "dare greatly" every time we make choices that challenge the social climate of scarcity.

The counterapproach to living in scarcity is not about abundance. In fact, I think abundance and scarcity are two sides of the same coin. The opposite of "never enough" isn't abundance or "more than you could ever imagine." The opposite of scarcity is enough, or what I call *Wholeheartedness*. As I explained in the Introduction, there are many tenets of Wholeheartedness, but at its very core is vulnerability and worthiness: facing uncertainty, exposure, and emotional risks, and knowing that I am enough.

If you go back to the three sets of questions about scarcity that I just posed and ask yourself if you'd be willing to be vulnerable or to dare greatly in any setting defined by these values, the answer for most of us is a resounding no. If you ask yourself if these are conditions conducive to cultivating worthiness, the answer is again no. *The greatest casualties of a scarcity culture are our willingness to own our vulnerabilities and our ability to engage with the world from a place of worthiness.*

After doing this work for the past twelve years and watching scarcity ride roughshod over our families, organizations, and communities, I'd say the one thing we have in common is that we're sick of feeling afraid. We all want to be brave. We want to dare greatly. We're tired of the national conversation centering on "What should we fear?" and "Who should we blame?"

In the next chapter we'll talk about the vulnerability myths that fuel scarcity and how courage starts with showing up and letting ourselves be seen.

CHAPTER 2
DEBUNKING
THE VULNERABILITY
MYTHS

Yes, we are totally exposed when we are vulnerable. Yes, we are in the torture chamber that we call uncertainty. And, yes, we're taking a huge emotional risk when we allow ourselves to be vulnerable. But there's no equation where taking risks, braving uncertainty, and opening ourselves up to emotional exposure equals weakness.

MYTH #1: "VULNERABILITY IS WEAKNESS."

The perception that vulnerability is weakness is the most widely accepted myth about vulnerability *and* the most dangerous. When we spend our lives pushing away and protecting ourselves from feeling vulnerable or from being perceived as too emotional, we feel contempt when others are less capable or willing to mask feelings, suck it up, and soldier on. We've come to the point where, rather than respecting and appreciating the courage and daring behind vulnerability, we let our fear and discomfort become judgment and criticism.

Vulnerability isn't good or bad: It's not what we call a dark emotion, nor is it always a light, positive experience. Vulnerability is the core of all emotions and feelings. To feel is to be vulnerable. To believe vulnerability is weakness is to believe that feeling is weakness. To foreclose on our emotional life out of a fear that the costs will be too high is to walk away from the very thing that gives purpose and meaning to living.

Our rejection of vulnerability often stems from our associating it with dark emotions like fear, shame, grief, sadness, and disappointment—emotions that we don't want to discuss, even when they profoundly affect the way we live, love, work, and even lead. What most of us fail to understand and what took me a decade of research to learn is that vulnerability is also the cradle of the emotions and experiences that we crave. Vulnerability is the birthplace of love, belonging, joy, courage, empathy, and creativity. It is the source of hope, empathy, accountability, and authenticity. If we want greater clarity in our purpose or deeper and more meaningful spiritual lives, vulnerability is the path.

I know this is hard to believe, especially when we've spent our lives thinking that vulnerability and weakness are synonymous, but it's true. **I define vulnerability as uncertainty, risk, and emotional exposure.** With that definition in mind, let's think about love. Waking up every day and loving someone who may or may not love us back, whose safety we can't ensure, who may stay in our lives or may leave without a moment's notice, who may be loyal to the day they die or betray us tomorrow—that's vulnerability. Love is uncertain. It's incredibly risky. And loving someone leaves us emotionally exposed. Yes, it's scary and yes, we're open to being hurt, but can you imagine your life without loving or being loved?

To put our art, our writing, our photography, our ideas out into the world with no assurance of acceptance or appreciation—that's also vulnerability. To let ourselves sink into the joyful moments of our lives even though we know that they are fleeting, even though the world tells us not to be too happy lest we invite disaster—that's an intense form of vulnerability.

The profound danger is that, as noted above, we start to think of *feeling* as weakness. With the exception of anger (which is a secondary emotion, one that only serves as a socially acceptable mask for many of the more difficult underlying emotions we feel), we're losing our tolerance for emotion and hence for vulnerability.

It starts to make sense that we dismiss vulnerability as weakness only when we realize that we've confused *feeling* with *failing* and *emotions* with *liabilities*. If we want to reclaim the essential emotional part of our lives and reignite our passion and purpose, we have to learn how to own and engage with our vulnerability and how to feel the emotions that come with it. For some of us, it's new learning, and for others it's relearning. Either way, the research taught me that the best place to start is with defining, recognizing, and understanding vulnerability.

What really brings the definition of vulnerability up close and personal are the examples people shared when I asked them to finish this sentence stem: "Vulnerability is _____." Here are some of the replies:

- Sharing an unpopular opinion

- Standing up for myself

- Asking for help

- Saying no

- Starting my own business

- Helping my thirty-seven-year-old wife with Stage 4 breast cancer make decisions about her will

- Initiating sex with my wife

- Initiating sex with my husband

- Hearing how much my son wants to make first chair in the orchestra and encouraging him while knowing that it's probably not going to happen

- Calling a friend whose child just died

- Signing up my mom for hospice care

- The first date after my divorce

- Saying, "I love you," first and not knowing if I'm going to be loved back

- Writing something I wrote or a piece of art that I made

- Getting promoted and not knowing if I'm going to succeed

- Getting fired

- Falling in love

- Trying something new

- Bringing my new boyfriend home

- Getting pregnant after three miscarriages

- Waiting for the biopsy to come back

- Reaching out to my son who is going through a difficult divorce

- Exercising in public, especially when I don't know what I'm doing and I'm out of shape

- Admitting I'm afraid

- Stepping up to the plate again after a series of strikeouts

- Telling my CEO that we won't make payroll next month

- Laying off employees

- Presenting my product to the world and getting no response

- Standing up for myself and for friends when someone else is critical or gossiping

- Being accountable

- Asking for forgiveness

- Having faith

Do these sound like weaknesses? Does showing up to be with someone in deep struggle sound like a weakness? Is accepting accountability weak? Is stepping up to the plate after striking out a sign of weakness? NO. *Vulnerability sounds like truth and feels like courage.* Truth and courage aren't always comfortable, but they're never weakness.

Yes, we are totally exposed when we are vulnerable. Yes, we are in the torture chamber that we call uncertainty. And, yes, we're taking a huge emotional risk when we allow ourselves to be vulnerable. But there's no equation where taking risks, braving uncertainty, and opening ourselves up to emotional exposure equals weakness.

When we asked the question "How does vulnerability feel?" the answers were equally as powerful:

- It's taking off the mask and hoping the real me isn't too disappointing.

- Not sucking it in anymore.

- It's where courage and fear meet.

- You are halfway across a tightrope, and moving forward and going back are both just as scary.

- Sweaty palms and a racing heart.

- Scary and exciting; terrifying and hopeful.

- Taking off a straitjacket.

- Going out on a limb—a very, very high limb.

- Taking the first step toward what you fear the most.

- Being all in.

- It feels so awkward and scary, but it makes me human and alive.

- A lump in my throat and a knot in my chest.

- The terrifying point on a roller coaster when you're about to tip over the edge and take the plunge.

- Freedom and liberation.

- It feels like fear, every single time.

- Panic, anxiety, fear, and hysteria, followed by freedom, pride, and amazement—then a little more panic.

- Baring your belly in the face of the enemy.

- Infinitely terrifying and achingly necessary.

- I know it's happening when I feel the need to strike first before I'm struck.

- It feels like free-falling.

- Like the time between hearing a gunshot and waiting to see if you're hit.

- Letting go of control.

And the answer that appeared over and over in all of our efforts to better understand vulnerability? *Naked.*

- Vulnerability is like being naked onstage and hoping for applause rather than laughter.

- It's being naked when everyone else is fully clothed.

- It feels like the naked dream: You're in the airport and you're stark naked.

When discussing vulnerability, it is helpful to look at the definition and etymology of the word *vulnerable*. According to the Merriam-Webster Dictionary, the word *vulnerability* is derived from the Latin word *vulnerare*, meaning "to wound." The definition includes "capable of being wounded" and "open to attack or damage." Merriam-Webster defines *weakness* as the inability to withstand attack or wounding. Just from a linguistic perspective, it's clear that these are very different concepts, and in fact, one could argue that weakness often stems from a lack of vulnerability—when we don't acknowledge how and where we're tender, we're more at risk of being hurt.

Psychology and social psychology have produced very persuasive evidence on the importance of acknowledging vulnerabilities. From the field of health psychology, studies show that perceived vulnerability, meaning the ability to acknowledge our risks and exposure, greatly increases our chances of adhering to some kind of positive health regimen. In order to get patients to comply with prevention routines, they must work on perceived vulnerability. And what makes this really interesting is that the critical issue is not about our actual level of vulnerability, but the level at which we *acknowledge* our vulnerabilities around a certain illness or threat.

From the field of social psychology, influence-and-persuasion researchers, who examine how people are affected by advertising and marketing, conducted a series of studies on vulnerability. They found that the participants who thought they were not susceptible or vulnerable to deceptive advertising were, in fact, the most vulnerable. The researchers' explanation for this phenomenon says it all: **"Far from being an effective shield, the illusion of invulnerability undermines the very response that would have supplied genuine protection."**

One of the most anxiety-provoking experiences of my career was speaking at the TED Conference in Long Beach that I referenced in the Introduction. In addition to all of the normal fears associated with giving a filmed, eighteen-minute talk in front of an intensely successful and high-expectation audience, I was the closing speaker for the entire event. For three days I sat and watched some of the most amazing and provocative talks that I've ever seen.

After each talk I slumped a little lower in my chair with the realization that in order for my talk "to work" I'd have to give up trying to do it like everyone else and I'd have to connect with the audience. I desperately wanted to see a talk that I could copy or use as a template, but the talks that resonated the most strongly with me didn't follow a format, they were just genuine. This meant that I'd have to be me. I'd have to be vulnerable and open. I'd need to walk away from my script and look people in the eye. I'd have to be naked. And, oh, my God . . . I hate naked. I have recurring nightmares about naked.

When I finally walked onto the stage the first thing I did was make eye contact with several people in the audience. I asked the stage managers to bring up the houselights so I could see people. I needed to feel connected. Simply seeing people as people rather than "the audience" reminded me that the challenges that scare me—like being naked—scare everyone else. I think that's why empathy can be conveyed without speaking a word—it just takes looking into someone's eyes and seeing yourself reflected back in an engaged way.

During my talk I asked the audience two questions that reveal so much about the many paradoxes that define vulnerability. First I asked, "How many of you struggle to be vulnerable because you think of vulnerability as weakness?" Hands shot up across the room. Then I asked, "When you watched people on this stage being vulnerable, how many of you thought it was courageous?" Again, hands shot up across the room.

We love seeing raw truth and openness in other people, but we're afraid to let them see it in us. We're afraid that our truth isn't enough—that what we have to offer isn't enough without the bells and whistles, without editing, and impressing. I was afraid to walk on that stage and show the audience my kitchen-table self—these people were too important, too successful, too famous. My kitchen-table self is too messy, too imperfect, too unpredictable.

Here's the crux of the struggle:

I want to experience your vulnerability but I don't want to be vulnerable.

Vulnerability is courage in you and inadequacy in me.
I'm drawn to your vulnerability but repelled by mine.

As I walked on the stage, I focused my thoughts on Steve, who was sitting in the audience, my sisters back in Texas, and some friends who were watching live from TEDActive—an offsite location. I also drew courage from something that I learned at TED—a very unexpected lesson on failure. The vast majority of folks whom Steve and I met during the three days leading up to my talk spoke openly about failing. It wasn't unusual for someone to tell you about the two or three ventures or inventions that had failed as they explained their work or talked about their passions. I was blown away and inspired.

I took a deep breath and recited my vulnerability prayer as I waited for my turn: *Give me the courage to show up and let myself be seen.* Then, seconds before I was introduced, I thought about a paperweight on my desk that reads, "What would you attempt to do if you knew you could not fail?" I pushed that question out of my head to make room for a new question. As I walked up to the stage, I literally whispered aloud, "What's worth doing even if I fail?"

I honestly don't remember much of what I said, but when it was over I was back knee-deep in the vulnerability hangover AGAIN! Was the risk worth it? Absolutely. I am passionate about my work and I believe in what I've learned from my research participants. I believe honest conversations about vulnerability and shame can change the world. Both of the talks are flawed and imperfect, but I walked into the arena and gave it my best shot. The willingness to show up changes us. It makes us a little braver each time. And, I'm not sure how one measures the success or failure of a talk, but the minute I was done I knew that even if it flopped or drew criticism, it had been totally worth doing.

In the song "Hallelujah," Leonard Cohen writes, "Love is not a victory march, it's a cold and it's a broken hallelujah." Love is a form of vulnerability and if you replace the word *love* with *vulnerability* in that line, it's just as true. From calling a friend who's experienced a terrible tragedy to starting your own business, from feeling terrified to experiencing liberation, vulnerability is life's great dare. It's life asking, "Are you all in? Can you value your own vulnerability as much as you value it in others?" Answering yes to these questions is not weakness: It's courage beyond measure. It's daring greatly. And often the result of daring greatly isn't a victory march as much as it is a quiet sense of freedom mixed with a little battle fatigue.

MYTH #2: "I DON'T DO VULNERABILITY"

> When we were children, we used to think that when we were grown up we would no longer be vulnerable. But to grow up is to accept vulnerability. To be alive is to be vulnerable.
>
> —Madeleine L'Engle

The definition and examples that you just read make busting the second vulnerability myth a lot easier. I can't tell you how many times I've heard people say, "Interesting topic, but I don't do vulnerability." It's often buttressed by a gender or professional explanation: "I'm an engineer—we hate vulnerability." "I'm a lawyer—we eat vulnerability for breakfast." "Guys don't do vulnerability." Trust me, I get it. I'm not a guy or an engineer or a lawyer, but I've spoken these exact words a hundred times. Unfortunately, there is no "get out of vulnerability free" card. We can't opt out of the uncertainty, risk, and emotional exposure that's woven through our daily experiences. Life is vulnerable.

Look back at the list of examples. These are the challenges of being alive, of being in a relationship, of being connected. Even if we choose to stay out of relationships and opt for disconnection as a form of protection, we're still alive and that means vulnerability happens. When we operate from the belief that we "don't do vulnerability" it's extremely helpful to ask ourselves the following questions. If we truly don't know the answers, we can bravely ask someone with whom we are close—they'll probably have an answer (even if we don't want to hear it):

1. "What do I do when I feel emotionally exposed?"
2. "How do I behave when I'm feeling very uncomfortable and uncertain?"
3. "How willing am I to take emotional risks?"

Before I started doing this work, my honest answers would have been:

1. Scared, angry, judgmental, controlling, perfecting, manufacturing certainty.
2. Scared, angry, judgmental, controlling, perfecting, manufacturing certainty.
3. At work, very unwilling if criticism, judgment, blame, or shame was possible. Taking emotional risks with the people I love was always mired in fear of something bad happening—a total joy killer that we'll explore in the "Armory" chapter.

This questioning process helps because, as you can see from my answers, regardless of our willingness to do vulnerability, *it does us.* When we pretend that we can avoid vulnerability we engage in behaviors that are often inconsistent with who we want to be. Experiencing vulnerability isn't a choice—the only choice we have is how we're going to respond when we are confronted with uncertainty, risk, and emotional exposure. As a huge fan of the band Rush, this seems like the perfect place to throw in a quote from their song "Freewill": "If you choose not to decide, you still have made a choice."

In Chapter 4 we'll take a closer look at the conscious and unconscious behaviors we use to protect ourselves when we believe we're "not doing vulnerability."

MYTH #3: VULNERABILITY IS LETTING IT ALL HANG OUT

One line of questioning that I often get is about our "let it all hang out" culture. *Can't there be too much vulnerability? Isn't there such a thing as oversharing?* These questions are inevitably followed by examples from celebrity culture. *What about when Movie Star X tweeted about her husband's suicide attempt? Or what about reality TV stars who share the intimate details of their lives and their children's lives with the world?*

Vulnerability is based on mutuality and requires boundaries and trust. It's not oversharing, it's not purging, it's not indiscriminate disclosure, and it's not celebrity-style social media information dumps. Vulnerability is about sharing our feelings and our experiences with people who have earned the right to hear them. Being vulnerable and open is mutual and an integral part of the trust-building process.

We can't always have guarantees in place before we risk sharing; however, we don't bare our souls the first time we meet someone. We don't lead with "Hi, my name is Brené, and here's my darkest struggle." That's not vulnerability. That may be desperation or woundedness or even attention-seeking, but it's not vulnerability. Why? Because sharing appropriately, with boundaries, means sharing with people with whom we've developed relationships that can bear the weight of our story. The result of this mutually respectful vulnerability is increased connection, trust, and engagement.

Vulnerability without boundaries leads to disconnection, distrust, and disengagement. In fact, as we'll explore in Chapter 4, "letting it all hang out" or boundaryless disclosure is one way we protect ourselves from real vulnerability. And the TMI (too much information) issue is not even a case of "too much vulnerability"—vulnerability is bankrupt on its own terms when people move from *being* vulnerable to *using* vulnerability to deal with unmet needs, get attention, or engage in the shock-and-awe behaviors that are so commonplace in today's culture.

To more effectively dispel the myth that vulnerability is a secret-sharing-free-for-all, let's examine the issue of trust.

When I talk to groups about the importance of being vulnerable, there's always a flood of questions about the need for trust:

"How do I know if I can trust someone enough to be vulnerable?"

"I'll only be vulnerable with someone if I'm sure they won't turn on me."

"How can you tell who's got your back?"

"How do we build trust with people?"

The good news is that the answers to these questions emerged from the data. The bad news is that it's a chicken-or-the-egg issue: We need to feel trust to be vulnerable and we need to be vulnerable in order to trust.

There is no trust test, no scoring system, no green light that tells us that it's safe to let ourselves be seen. The research participants described trust as a slow-building, layered process that happens over time. In our family, we refer to trust as "the Marble Jar."

In the middle of third grade, Ellen had her first experience with betrayal. In many elementary school settings, third grade is a big move. Students are no longer clustered with the K–2 crowd; they're now navigating the Grade 3–5 group. During recess, she had confided in a friend from her class about a funny, slightly embarrassing thing that had happened to her earlier in the day. By lunchtime, all of the girls in her peer group knew her secret and were giving her a hard time. It was an important lesson, but also a painful one, because up to that point she had never considered the possibility that someone would do that.

When she came home, she burst into tears and told me that she was never going to tell anyone anything again. Her feelings were so hurt. Listening, I felt my heart aching for her. To make matters worse, Ellen told me that the girls were still laughing at her when they returned to the classroom, so much so that her teacher separated them and took some marbles out of the marble jar.

Ellen's teacher had a large, clear glass vase that she and the kids referred to as "the marble jar." She kept a bag of colored marbles next to the jar, and whenever the class was collectively making good choices, she would throw some marbles into the jar. Whenever the class was acting out, breaking rules, or not listening, the teacher would take marbles out of the jar. If and when the marbles made it to the top of the jar, the students would be rewarded with a celebration party.

As much as I wanted to pull Ellen close and whisper, "Not sharing with those girls is a great idea! That way they'll never hurt ~~us~~ you again," I put my fears and anger aside, and started trying to figure out how to talk to her about trust and connection. As I was searching for the right way to translate my own experiences of trust, and what I was learning about trust from the research, I thought, *Ah, the marble jar. Perfect.*

I told Ellen to think about her friendships as marble jars. Whenever someone supports you, or is kind to you, or sticks up for you, or honors what you share with them as private, you put marbles in the jar. When people are mean, or disrespectful, or share your secrets, marbles come out. When I asked her if it made sense, she nodded her head with excitement and said, "I've got marble jar friends! I've got marble jar friends!"

When I asked her to tell me about it, she described four friends whom she could always count on, who knew some of her secrets and would never tell, and who told her some of their secrets too. She said, "These are the friends who ask me to sit with them, even if they've been asked to sit at the popular kids' table."

It was such a great moment for both of us. When I asked her how her marble jar friends became marble jar friends, she thought about it for a minute and replied, "I'm not sure. How did your marble jar friends get their marbles?" After thinking about it for a while, we both started blurting out our answers. Some of hers were:

They keep our secrets.

They tell us their secrets.

They remember my birthday!

They know who Oma and Opa are.

They always make sure I'm included in fun things.

They know when I'm sad and ask me why.

When I miss school because I'm sick, they ask their moms to call to check on me.

And mine? Exactly the same (except for me, Oma and Opa are Deanne and David, my mom and stepdad). When my mom comes to Ellen or Charlie's events, it's a great feeling to hear one of my friends say, "Hey, Deanne! Good to see you." I always think, *She remembered my mom's name. She cares. She's paying attention.*

Trust is built one marble at a time.

The chicken-or-the-egg dilemma comes into play when we think about the investment and leap that people in relationships have to make before the building process ever begins. The teacher didn't say, "I'm not buying a jar and marbles until I know that the class can collectively make good choices." The jar was there on the first day of school. In fact, by the end of the first day, she had already filled the bottom with a layer of marbles. The kids didn't say, "We're not going to make good choices because we don't believe you'll put marbles in the jar." They worked hard and enthusiastically engaged with the marble jar idea based on their teacher's word.

One of my favorite scholars in the field of relationships is

John Gottman. He's considered the country's foremost couples researcher because of the power and accessibility of his pioneering work on how we connect and build relationships. His book *The Science of Trust: Emotional Attunement for Couples* is an insightful and wise book on the anatomy of trust and trust building. In an article on the University of California–Berkeley's "Greater Good" website (www.greatergood.berkeley.edu), Gottman describes trust building with our partners in a manner totally consistent with what I found in my research and what Ellen and I call the marble jar:

> What I've found through research is that trust is built in very small moments, which I call "sliding door" moments, after the movie *Sliding Doors*. In any interaction, there is a possibility of connecting with your partner or turning away from your partner.
>
> Let me give you an example of that from my own relationship. One night, I really wanted to finish a mystery novel. I thought I knew who the killer was, but I was anxious to find out. At one point in the night, I put the novel on my bedside and walked into the bathroom.
>
> As I passed the mirror, I saw my wife's face in the reflection, and she looked sad, brushing her hair. There was a sliding door moment.
>
> I had a choice. I could sneak out of the bathroom and think, *I don't want to deal with her sadness tonight; I want to read my novel.* But instead, because I'm a sensitive researcher of relationships, I decided to go into the bathroom. I took the brush from her hair and asked,

"What's the matter, baby?" And she told me why she was sad.

Now, at that moment, I was building trust; I was there for her. I was connecting with her rather than choosing to think only about what I wanted. These are the moments, we've discovered, that build trust.

One such moment is not that important, but if you're always choosing to turn away, then trust erodes in a relationship—very gradually, very slowly.

When we think about betrayal in terms of the marble jar metaphor, most of us think of someone we trust doing something so terrible that it forces us to grab the jar and dump out every single marble. What's the worst betrayal of trust you can think of? He sleeps with my best friend. She lies about where the money went. He/she chooses someone over me. Someone uses my vulnerability against me (an act of emotional treason that causes most of us to slam the entire jar to the ground rather than just dumping the marbles). All terrible betrayals, definitely, but there is a particular sort of betrayal that is more insidious and equally corrosive to trust.

In fact, this betrayal usually happens long before the other ones. I'm talking about the betrayal of disengagement. Of not caring. Of letting the connection go. Of not being willing to devote time and effort to the relationship. The word *betrayal* evokes experiences of cheating, lying, breaking a confidence, failing to defend us to someone else who's gossiping about us, and not choosing us over other people. These behaviors are certainly betrayals, but they're not the only form of betrayal. If I had to choose the form of betrayal that emerged most frequently from my research and that was the most dangerous in terms of corroding the trust connection, I would say disengagement.

When the people we love or with whom we have a deep connection stop caring, stop paying attention, stop investing, and stop fighting for the relationship, trust begins to slip away and hurt starts seeping in. Disengagement triggers shame and our greatest fears—the fears of being abandoned, unworthy, and unlovable. What can make this covert betrayal so much more dangerous than something like a lie or an affair is that we can't point to the source of our pain—there's no event, no obvious evidence of brokenness. It can feel crazy-making.

We may tell a disengaged partner, "You don't seem to care anymore," but without "evidence" of this, the response is "I'm home from work every night by six P.M. I tuck in the kids. I'm taking the boys to Little League. What do you want from me?" Or at work, we think, *Why am I not getting feedback? Tell me you love it! Tell me it sucks! Just tell me something so I know you remember that I work here!*

With children, actions speak louder than words. When we stop requesting invitations into their lives by asking about their day, asking them to tell us about their favorite songs, wondering how their friends are doing, then children feel pain and fear (and not relief, despite how our teenagers may act). Because they can't articulate how they feel about our disengagement when we stop making an effort with them, they show us by acting out, thinking, *This will get their attention.*

Like trust, most experiences of betrayal happen slowly, one marble at a time. In fact, the overt or "big" betrayals that I mentioned before are more likely to happen after a period of disengagement and slowly eroding trust. What I've learned about trust professionally and what I've lived personally boils down to this:

Trust is a product of vulnerability that grows over time and requires work, attention, and full engagement. Trust isn't a grand gesture—it's a growing marble collection.

MYTH #4: WE CAN GO IT ALONE

Going it alone is a value we hold in high esteem in our culture, ironically even when it comes to cultivating connection. I get the appeal; I have that rugged individualism in my DNA. In fact, one of my very favorite break-up-kick-ass-no-one-can-hurt-me songs is Whitesnake's "Here I Go Again." If you're a person of a certain age, I'd put money down that you've rolled down the window and defiantly sung: "And here I go again on my own. . . . Like a drifter I was born to walk alone. . . ." If Whitesnake isn't your cup of tea, there are bootstrapping anthems in every imaginable genre. In reality, walking alone can feel miserable and depressing, but we admire the strength it conveys, and *going it alone* is revered in our culture.

Well, as much as I love the idea of walking alone down a lonely street of dreams, the vulnerability journey is *not* the kind of journey we can make alone. We need support. We need folks who will let us try on new ways of being without judging us. We need a hand to pull us up off the ground when we get kicked down in the arena (and if we live a courageous life, that will happen). Across the course of my research, participants were very clear about their need for support, encouragement, and sometimes professional help as they reengaged with vulnerability and their emotional lives. Most of us are good at giving help, but when it comes to vulnerability, we need to ask for help too.

In *The Gifts of Imperfection*, I write, "Until we can receive with an open heart, we are never really giving with an open heart. When we attach judgment to receiving help, we knowingly or unknowingly attach judgment to giving help." We all need help. I know I couldn't have done it without reinforcements that included my husband Steve, a great therapist, a stack of books a mile high, and friends and family members who were on a similar journey. Vulnerability begets vulnerability; courage is contagious.

There's actually some very persuasive leadership research that supports the idea that asking for support is critical, and that vulnerability and courage are contagious. In a 2011 *Harvard Business Review* article, Peter Fuda and Richard Badham use a series of metaphors to explore how leaders spark and sustain change. One of the metaphors is the snowball. The snowball starts rolling when a leader is willing to be vulnerable with his or her subordinates. Their research shows that this act of vulnerability is predictably perceived as courageous by team members and inspires others to follow suit.

Supporting the metaphor of the snowball is the story of Clynton, the managing director of a large German corporation who realized that his directive leadership style was preventing senior managers from taking initiative. The researchers explain, "He could have worked in private to change his behavior—but instead he stood up at an annual meeting of his top sixty managers, acknowledged his failings, and outlined both his personal and organizational roles. He admitted that he didn't have all of the answers and asked his team for help leading the company." Having studied the transformation that followed this event, the researchers report that Clynton's effectiveness surged, his team flourished, there were increases in initiative and innovation, and his organization went on to outperform much larger competitors.

Similar to the story above, my greatest personal and professional transformations happened when I started asking hard questions about how my fear of being vulnerable was holding me back and when I found the courage to share my struggles and ask for help. After running from vulnerability, I found that learning how to lean into the discomfort of uncertainty, risk, and emotional exposure was a painful process.

I did believe that I could opt out of feeling vulnerable, so when it happened—when the phone rang with unimaginable news; or when I was scared; or when I loved so fiercely that rather than feeling gratitude and joy I could only prepare for loss—I controlled things. I managed situations and micromanaged the people around me. I performed until there was no energy left to feel. I made what was uncertain certain, no matter what the cost. I stayed so busy that the truth of my hurting and my fear could never catch up. I looked brave on the outside and felt scared on the inside.

Slowly I learned that this shield was too heavy to lug around, and that the only thing it really did was keep me from knowing myself and letting myself be known. The shield required that I stay small and quiet behind it so as not to draw attention to my imperfections and vulnerabilities. It was exhausting.

I remember a very tender moment from that year, when Steve and I were lying on the floor watching Ellen do a series of crazy, arm-flinging, and knee-slapping dances and tumbles. I looked at Steve and said, "Isn't it funny how I just love her that much more for being so vulnerable and uninhibited and goofy. I could never do that. Can you imagine knowing that you're loved like that?" Steve looked at me and said, "I love you exactly like that." Honestly, as someone who rarely risked vulnerability and always steered clear of silly or goofy, it never dawned on me that adults could love each other like that; that I could be loved for my vulnerabilities, not despite them.

All of the love and support I received—especially from Steve and Diana, my therapist—allowed me to slowly begin to take more risks, to show up at work and at home in new ways. I took more chances and tried new things, like story-telling. I learned how to set new boundaries and say no, even when I was terrified that I was going to piss off a friend or squander a professional opportunity that I'd regret. *So far, I haven't regretted a single no.*

Going back to Roosevelt's "Man in the Arena" speech, I also learned that the people who love me, the people I really depend on, were never the critics who were pointing at me while I stumbled. They weren't in the bleachers at all. They were with me in the arena. Fighting for me and with me.

Nothing has transformed my life more than realizing that it's a waste of time to evaluate my worthiness by weigh-ing the reaction of the people in the stands. The people who love me and will be there regardless of the outcome are within arm's reach. This realization changed everything. That's the wife and mother and friend that I now strive to be. I want our home to be a place where we can be our bravest selves and our most fearful selves. Where we practice difficult conversations and share our shaming moments from school and work. I want to look at Steve and my kids and say, "I'm with you. In the arena. And when we fail, we'll fail together, while daring greatly." We simply can't learn to be more vulnerable and courageous on our own. Sometimes our first and greatest dare is asking for support.

CHAPTER 3

UNDERSTANDING AND COMBATING SHAME

(AKA, GREMLIN NINJA WARRIOR TRAINING)

Shame derives its power from being unspeakable. That's why it loves perfectionists—it's so easy to keep us quiet. If we cultivate enough awareness about shame to name it and speak to it, we've basically cut it off at the knees. Shame hates having words wrapped around it. If we speak shame, it begins to wither. Just the way exposure to light was deadly for the gremlins, language and story bring light to shame and destroy it.

VULNERABILITY AND SHAME IN ONE BOOK! ARE YOU TRYING TO KILL US?
OR
DEFENSE AGAINST THE DARK ARTS

Last year, after I had finished a talk on Wholehearted families, a man approached me on the stage. He stuck out his hand and said, "I just want to say thank you." I shook his hand and offered a kind smile as he looked down at the floor. I could tell that he was fighting back tears.

He took a deep breath and said, "I have to tell you that I really didn't want to come tonight. I tried to get out of it, but my wife made me."

I chuckled. "Yeah, I get that a lot."

"I couldn't understand why she was so excited. I told her that I couldn't think of a worse way to spend a Thursday night than listening to a shame researcher. She said that it was really important to her and I had to stop complaining, otherwise I'd ruin it for her." He paused for a few seconds, then surprised me by asking, "Are you a *Harry Potter* fan?"

I stalled for a second while I tried to connect everything he was saying. When I finally gave up, I answered his question. "Yes, I am a huge fan. I've read all of the books several times, and I've watched and rewatched the movies. I'm hardcore. Why?"

He looked a little embarrassed before he explained, "Well, I didn't know anything about you, and as my dread built up about coming tonight, I kept picturing you as Snape. I thought you'd be scary. I thought you'd be wearing all black and that you'd talk slowly and in a deep, haunting voice—like the world was ending."

I laughed so hard that I almost spit out the water I was drinking. "I love Snape! I'm not sure that I want to look like him, but he's my favorite character." I immediately glanced over at my purse, which was still tucked under the bottom of the podium. In it my keys were (and are) attached to my beloved LEGO Snape keychain.

We shared a laugh about his Snape projection, then things got more serious. "What you said really made sense to me. Especially the part about us being so afraid of the dark stuff. What's the quote that you shared with the picture of the twinkle lights?"

"Oh, the twinkle light quote. It's one of my favorites: 'Only when we're brave enough to explore the darkness will we discover the infinite power of our light.'"

He nodded. "Yes! That one! I'm sure that's why I didn't want to come. It's crazy how much energy we spend trying to avoid these hard topics when they're really the only ones that can set us free. I was shamed a lot growing up and I don't want to do that to my three kids. I want them to know they're enough. I don't want them to be afraid to talk about the hard shit with us. I want them to be shame resilient."

At this point we were both teary-eyed. I reached up and did that awkward "are you a hugger?" gesture, then I gave him a big ol' hug. After we let go of our this-stuff-is-hard-but-we-can-do-it embrace, he looked at me and said, "I'm pretty bad at vulnerability, but I'm really good at shame. Is getting past shame necessary for getting to vulnerability?"

"Yes. Shame resilience is key to embracing our vulnerability. We can't let ourselves be seen if we're terrified by what people might think. Often 'not being good at vulnerability' means that we're damn good at shame."

As I stumbled for better language to explain how shame stops us from being vulnerable and connected, I remembered my very favorite exchange from *Harry Potter*. "Do you remember when Harry was worried that he might be bad because he was angry all of the time and had dark feelings?"

He enthusiastically answered, "Yes! Of course! The conversation with Sirius Black! That's the moral of the entire story."

"Exactly! Sirius told Harry to listen to him very carefully, then he said, 'You're not a bad person. You're a very good person who bad things have happened to. Besides, the world isn't split into good people and Death Eaters. We've all got both light and dark inside us. What matters is the part we choose to act on. That's who we really are.'"

"I get it," he sighed.

"We all have shame. We all have good and bad, dark and light, inside of us. But if we don't come to terms with our shame, our struggles, we start believing that there's something wrong with us—that we're bad, flawed, not good enough—and even worse, we start acting on those beliefs. If we want to be fully engaged, to be connected, we have to be vulnerable. In order to be vulnerable, we need to develop resilience to shame."

At this point, his wife was waiting by the stage stairs. He thanked me, gave me another quick hug, and walked away.

Just as he reached the bottom of the stairs, he turned back and said, "You may not be Snape, but you're a damn good Defense Against the Dark Arts teacher!"

It was a conversation and a moment that I'll never forget. On the way home that night, I thought about a line from one of the books where Harry Potter was detailing the fate of several unsuccessful Defense Against the Dark Arts teachers: "One sacked, one dead, one lost his memory, and one was locked in a trunk for nine months." I remember thinking, "Sounds about right."

I won't go on with the *Harry Potter* metaphor because I'm sure there's one or two of you out there who haven't had the chance to read the books or see the films, but I have to say that J. K. Rowling's incredible imagination has made teaching shame a lot easier and way more fun. The allegorical power of *Harry Potter* lends itself to talking about everything from the struggle between light and dark to the hero's journey and why vulnerability and love are the truest marks of courage. Having spent so long trying to describe and define unnamed emotions and experiences, I find that *Harry Potter* has given me a treasure trove of characters, monsters, and images to use in my teaching. For that, I'll be forever grateful.

I didn't set out to become a wild-eyed shame evangelist or a Defense Against the Dark Arts teacher, but after spending the past decade studying the corrosive effect that shame has on how we live, love, parent, work, and lead, I've found myself practically screaming from the top of my lungs, "Yes, shame is tough to talk about. But the conversation isn't nearly as dangerous as what we're creating with our silence! We all experience shame. We're all afraid to talk about it. And, the less we talk about it, the more we have it."

We have to be vulnerable if we want more courage; if we want to dare greatly. But as I told my *Harry Potter* friend, how can we let ourselves be seen if shame has us terrified of what people might think?

Let me give you an example.

You've designed a product or written an article or created a piece of art that you want to share with a group of friends. Sharing something that you've created is a vulnerable but essential part of engaged and Wholehearted living. It's the epitome of daring greatly. But because of how you were raised or how you approach the world, you've knowingly or unknowingly attached your self-worth to how your product or art is received. In simple terms, if they love it, you're worthy; if they don't, you're worthless.

One of two things happens at this point in the process:

1. Once you realize that your self-worth is hitched to what you've produced or created, it's unlikely that you'll share it, or if you do, you'll strip away a layer or two of the juiciest creativity and innovation to make the revealing less risky. There's too much on the line to just put your wildest creations out there.

2. If you do share it in its most creative form and the reception doesn't meet your expectations, you're crushed. Your offering is no good and you're no good. The chances of soliciting feedback, reengaging, and going back to the drawing board are slim. You shut down. Shame tells you that you shouldn't have even tried. Shame tells you that you're not good enough and you should have known better.

If you're wondering what happens if you attach your self-worth to your art or your product and people love it, let me answer that from personal and professional experience. You're in even deeper trouble. Everything shame needs to hijack and control your life is in place. You've handed over your self-worth to what people think. It's panned out a couple of times, but now it feels a lot like Hotel California: You can check in, but you can never leave. You're officially a prisoner of "pleasing, performing, and perfecting."

With an awareness of shame and strong shame resilience skills, this scenario is completely different. You still want folks to like, respect, and even admire what you've created, but your self-worth is not on the table. You know that you are far more than a painting, an innovative idea, an effective pitch, a good sermon, or a high Amazon.com ranking. Yes, it will be disappointing and difficult if your friends or colleagues don't share your enthusiasm, or if things don't go well, but this effort is about what you do, not who you are. Regardless of the outcome, you've already dared greatly, and that's totally aligned with your values; with who you want to be.

When our self-worth isn't on the line, we are far more willing to be courageous and risk sharing our raw talents and gifts. From my research with families, schools, and organizations, it's clear that shame-resilient cultures nurture folks who are much more open to soliciting, accepting, and incorporating feedback. These cultures also nurture engaged, tenacious people who expect to have to try and try again to get it right—people who are much more willing to get innovative and creative in their efforts.

A sense of worthiness inspires us to be vulnerable, share openly, and persevere. Shame keeps us small, resentful, and afraid. In shame-prone cultures, where parents, leaders, and

administrators consciously or unconsciously encourage people to connect their self-worth to what they produce, I see
disengagement, blame, gossip, stagnation, favoritism, and a
total dearth of creativity and innovation.

Peter Sheahan is an author, speaker, and CEO of
ChangeLabs™, a global consultancy building and delivering
large-scale behavioral change projects for clients such as Apple
and IBM. Pete and I had the chance to work together last summer and I think his perspective on shame is spot on. Pete says,

> The secret killer of innovation is shame.
> You can't measure it, but it is there. Every
> time someone holds back on a new idea, fails
> to give their manager much needed feedback,
> and is afraid to speak up in front of a client
> you can be sure shame played a part. That
> deep fear we all have of being wrong, of being
> belittled and of feeling less than, is what stops
> us taking the very risks required to move our
> companies forward.
>
> If you want a culture of creativity and inno-
> vation, where sensible risks are embraced on
> both a market and individual level, start by de-
> veloping the ability of managers to cultivate
> an openness to vulnerability in their teams.
> And this, paradoxically perhaps, requires first
> that they are vulnerable themselves. This no-
> tion that the leader needs to be "in charge"
> and to "know all the answers" is both dated
> and destructive. Its impact on others is the
> sense that they know less, and that they are
> less than. A recipe for risk aversion if ever I

have heard it. Shame becomes fear. Fear leads
to risk aversion. Risk aversion kills innovation.

The bottom line is that *daring greatly* requires worthiness. Shame sends the gremlins to fill our heads with completely different messages of:

Dare not! You're not good enough!

Don't you dare get too big for your britches!

The term *gremlin*—as we are most familiar with it—comes from Steven Spielberg's 1984 horror comedy *Gremlins*. Gremlins are those evil little green tricksters who wreak havoc everywhere they go. They're manipulative monsters that derive pleasure from destruction. In many circles, including my own, the word *gremlin* has become synonymous with "shame tape."

For example, I was recently struggling to finish an article. I called a good friend to tell her about my writer's block, and she immediately responded by asking, "What are the gremlins saying?"

This is a very effective way of asking about the shame tapes—the messages of self-doubt and self-criticism that we carry around in our heads. My answer was "There are a few of them. One's saying that my writing sucks and that no one cares about these topics. Another one's telling me that I'm going to get criticized and I'll deserve it. And the big one keeps saying, 'Real writers don't struggle like this. Real writers don't dangle their modifiers.'"

Understanding our shame tapes or gremlins is critical to overcoming shame because we can't always point to a certain moment or a specific put-down at the hands of another person. Sometimes shame is the result of us playing the old recordings that were programmed when we were children or simply absorbed from the culture. My good friend and colleague Robert Hilliker says, "Shame started as a two-person experience, but as I got older I learned how to do shame all by myself." Sometimes when we dare to walk into the arena the greatest critic we face is ourselves.

Shame derives its power from being unspeakable. That's why it loves perfectionists—it's so easy to keep us quiet. If we cultivate enough awareness about shame to name it and speak to it, we've basically cut it off at the knees. Shame hates having words wrapped around it. If we speak shame, it begins to wither. Just the way exposure to light was deadly for the gremlins, language and story bring light to shame and destroy it.

Just like Roosevelt advised, when we dare greatly we will err and we will come up short again and again. There will be failures and mistakes and criticism. If we want to be able to move through the difficult disappointments, the hurt feelings, and the heartbreaks that are inevitable in a fully lived life, we can't equate defeat with being unworthy of love, belonging, and joy. If we do, we'll never show up and try again. Shame hangs out in the parking lot of the arena, waiting for us to come out defeated and determined to never take risks. It laughs and says, "I told you this was a mistake. I knew you weren't _____ enough." Shame resilience is the ability to say, "This hurts. This is disappointing, maybe even devastating. But success and recognition and approval are not the values that drive me. My value is courage and I was just courageous. You can move on, shame."

So, I'm not trying to kill you. I'm just saying, "We can't embrace vulnerability if shame is suffocating our sense of worthiness and connection." Strap yourself in, and let's get our heads and hearts around this experience called shame, so we can get about the business of truly living.

WHAT IS SHAME AND WHY IS IT SO HARD TO TALK ABOUT IT?

(If you're pretty sure that shame doesn't apply to you, keep reading; I'll clear that up in the next couple of pages.)

I start every talk, article, and chapter on shame with the Shame 1-2-3s, or the first three things that you need to know about shame, so you'll keep listening:

1. We all have it. Shame is universal and one of the most primitive human emotions that we experience. The only people who don't experience shame lack the capacity for empathy and human connection. Here's your choice: Fess up to experiencing shame or admit that you're a sociopath. *Quick note: This is the only time that shame seems like a good option.*
2. We're all afraid to talk about shame.
3. The less we talk about shame, the more control it has over our lives.

There are a couple of very helpful ways to think about shame. First, shame is the fear of disconnection. We are psychologically, emotionally, cognitively, and spiritually hard-wired for connection, love, and belonging. Connection, along with love and belonging (two expressions of connection), is why we are here, and it is what gives purpose and meaning to our lives. Shame is the fear of disconnection—it's the fear that something we've done or failed to do, an ideal that we've not lived up to, or a goal that we've not accomplished makes us unworthy of connection. *I'm not worthy or good enough for love, belonging, or connection.* I'm unlovable. I don't belong. Here's the definition of shame that emerged from my research:

Shame is the intensely painful feeling or experience of believing that we are flawed and therefore unworthy of love and belonging.

People often want to believe that shame is reserved for people who have survived an unspeakable trauma, but this is not true. Shame is something we all experience. And while it feels as if shame hides in our darkest corners, it actually tends to lurk in all of the familiar places. Twelve "shame categories" have emerged from my research:

- Appearance and body image

- Money and work

- Motherhood/fatherhood

- Family

- Parenting

- Mental and physical health

- Addiction

- Sex

- Aging

- Religion

- Surviving trauma

- Being stereotyped or labeled

Here are some of the responses we received when we asked people for an example of shame:

- Shame is getting laid off and having to tell my pregnant wife.

- Shame is having someone ask me, "When are you due?" when I'm not pregnant.

- Shame is hiding the fact that I'm in recovery.

- Shame is raging at my kids.

- Shame is bankruptcy.

- Shame is my boss calling me an idiot in front of the client.

- Shame is not making partner.

- Shame is my husband leaving me for my next-door neighbor.

- Shame is my wife asking me for a divorce and telling me that she wants children, but not with me.

- Shame is my DUI.

- Shame is infertility.

- Shame is telling my fiancé that my dad lives in France when in fact he's in prison.

- Shame is Internet porn.

- Shame is flunking out of school. Twice.

- Shame is hearing my parents fight through the walls and wondering if I'm the only one who feels this afraid.

Shame is real pain. The importance of social acceptance and connection is reinforced by our brain chemistry, and the pain that results from social rejection and disconnection is real pain. In a 2011 study funded by the National Institute of Mental Health and by the National Institute on Drug Abuse, researchers found that, as far as the brain is concerned, physical pain and intense experiences of social rejection hurt in the same way. So when I define shame as an intensely "painful" experience, I'm not kidding. Neuroscience advances confirm what we've known all along: Emotions can hurt and cause pain. And just as we often struggle to define physical pain, describing emotional pain is difficult. Shame is particularly hard because it hates having words wrapped around it. It hates being spoken.

UNTANGLING SHAME, GUILT, HUMILIATION, AND EMBARRASSMENT

In fact, as we work to understand shame, one of the simpler reasons that shame is so difficult to talk about is vocabulary. We often use the terms *embarrassment*, *guilt*, *humiliation*, and *shame* interchangeably. It might seem overly picky to stress the importance of using the appropriate term to describe an experience or emotion; however, it is much more than semantics.

How we experience these different emotions comes down to self-talk. How do we talk to ourselves about what's happening? The best place to start examining self-talk and untangling these four distinct emotions is with shame and guilt. The majority of shame researchers and clinicians agree that the difference between shame and guilt is best understood as the difference between "I am bad" and "I did something bad."

Guilt = I did something bad.

Shame = I am bad.

For example, let's say that you forgot that you made plans to meet a friend at noon for lunch. At 12:15 P.M., your friend calls from the restaurant to make sure you're okay. If your self-talk is "I'm such an idiot. I'm a terrible friend and a total loser"—that's shame. If, on the other hand, your self-talk is "I can't believe I *did* that. What a crappy thing *to do*"—that's guilt.

Here's what's interesting—especially for those who automatically think, *You should feel like a terrible friend!* or *A little shame will help you keep your act together next time*. When we feel shame, we are most likely to protect ourselves by blaming something or someone, rationalizing our lapse, offering a disingenuous apology, or hiding out. Rather than apologizing, we blame our friend and rationalize forgetting: "I told you I was really busy. This wasn't a good day for me." Or we apologize halfheartedly and think to ourselves, *Whatever. If she knew how busy I am, she'd be apologizing*. Or we see who is calling and don't answer the phone at all, and then when we finally can't stop dodging our friend, we lie: "Didn't you get my e-mail? I canceled in the morning. You should check your spam folder."

When we apologize for something we've done, make amends, or change a behavior that doesn't align with our values, guilt—not shame—is most often the driving force. We feel guilty when we hold up something we've done or failed to do against our values and find they don't match up. It's an uncomfortable feeling, but one that's helpful. The psychological discomfort, something similar to cognitive dissonance, is what motivates meaningful change. Guilt is just as powerful as shame, but its influence is positive, while shame's is destructive. In fact, in my research I found that shame corrodes the very part of us that believes we can change and do better.

We live in a world where most people still subscribe to

the belief that shame is a good tool for keeping people in line. Not only is this wrong, but it's dangerous. Shame is highly correlated with addiction, violence, aggression, depression, eating disorders, and bullying. Researchers don't find shame correlated with positive outcomes at all—there are no data to support that shame is a helpful compass for good behavior. In fact, shame is much more likely to be the cause of destructive and hurtful behaviors than it is to be the solution.

Again, it is human nature to want to feel worthy of love and belonging. When we experience shame, we feel disconnected and desperate for worthiness. When we're hurting, either full of shame or even just feeling the fear of shame, we are more likely to engage in self-destructive behaviors and to attack or shame others. In the chapters on parenting, leadership, and education, we'll explore how shame erodes our courage and fuels disengagement, and what we can do to cultivate cultures of worthiness, vulnerability, and shame resilience.

Humiliation is another word that we often confuse with *shame*. Donald Klein captures the difference between shame and humiliation when he writes, "People believe they deserve their shame; they do not believe they deserve their humiliation." If John is in a meeting with his colleagues and his boss, and his boss calls him a loser because of his inability to close a sale, John will probably experience that as either shame or humiliation.

If John's self-talk is "God, I am a loser. I'm a failure"—that's shame. If his self-talk is "Man, my boss is so out of control. This is ridiculous. I don't deserve this"—that's humiliation. Humiliation feels terrible and makes for a miserable work or home environment—and if it's ongoing, it can certainly become shame if we start to buy into the messaging. It is, however, still better than shame. Rather than internalizing the "loser" comment, John's saying to himself, "This isn't about me." When we do that, it's less likely that we'll shut down, act out, or fight back. We stay aligned with our values while trying to solve the problem.

Embarrassment is the least serious of the four emotions. It's normally fleeting and it can eventually be funny. The hallmark of embarrassment is that when we do something embarrassing, we don't feel alone. We know other folks have done the same thing and, like a blush, it will pass rather than define us.

Getting familiar with the language is an important start to understanding shame. It is part of the first element of what I call shame resilience.

I GET IT. SHAME IS BAD. SO WHAT DO WE DO ABOUT IT?

The answer is shame *resilience*. Note that shame *resistance* is not possible. As long as we care about connection, the fear of disconnection will always be a powerful force in our lives, and the pain caused by shame will always be real. But here's the great news. In all my studies, I've found that men and women with high levels of shame resilience have four things in common—I call them the elements of shame resilience. Learning to put these elements into action is what I call "Gremlin Ninja Warrior training."

We'll go through each of the four elements, but first I want to explain what I mean by shame resilience. I mean the ability to practice authenticity when we experience shame, to move through the experience without sacrificing our values, and to come out on the other side of the shame experience with more courage, compassion, and connection than we had going into it. Shame resilience is about moving from shame to empathy—the real antidote to shame.

If we can share our story with someone who responds with empathy and understanding, shame can't survive. Self-compassion is also critically important, but because shame is a social concept—it happens between people—it also heals best between people. A social wound needs a social balm, and empathy is that balm. Self-compassion is key because when we're able to be gentle with ourselves in the midst of shame, we're more likely to reach out, connect, and experience empathy.

To get to empathy, we have to first know what we're dealing with. Here are the four elements of shame resilience—the steps don't always happen in this order, but they always ultimately lead us to empathy and healing:

1. **Recognizing Shame and Understanding Its Triggers.** Shame is biology and biography. Can you physically recognize when you're in the grips of shame, feel your way through it, and figure out what messages and expectations triggered it?

2. **Practicing Critical Awareness.** Can you reality-check the messages and expectations that are driving your shame? Are they realistic? Attainable? Are they what you want to be or what you think others need/want from you?

3. **Reaching Out.** Are you owning and sharing your story? We can't experience empathy if we're not connecting.

4. **Speaking Shame.** Are you talking about how you feel and asking for what you need when you feel shame?

Shame resilience is a strategy for protecting connection—our connection with ourselves and our connections with the people we care about. But resilience requires cognition, or thinking, and that's where shame has a huge advantage. When shame descends, we almost always are hijacked by the limbic system. In other words, the prefrontal cortex, where we do all of our thinking and analyzing and strategizing, gives way to that primitive fight-or-flight part of our brain.

In his book *Incognito*, neuroscientist David Eagleman describes the brain as a "team of rivals." He writes, "There is an ongoing conversation among the different factions in your brain, each competing to control the single output channel of your behavior." He lays out the dominant two-party system of reason and emotion: "The rational system is the one that cares about analysis of things in the outside world, while the emotional system monitors the internal state and worries whether things are good or bad." Eagleman makes the case that because both parties are battling to control one output—behavior—emotions can tip the balance of decision making. I would say that's definitely true when the emotion is shame.

Our fight or flight strategies are effective for survival, not for reasoning or connection. And the pain of shame is enough to trigger that survival part of our brain that runs, hides, or comes out swinging. In fact, when I asked the research participants how they normally responded to shame before they started working on shame resilience, I heard many comments like these:

- "When I feel shame, I'm like a crazy person. I do stuff and say stuff I would normally never do or say."

- "Sometimes I just wish I could make other people feel as bad as I do. I just want to lash out and scream at everyone."

- "I get desperate when I feel shame. Like I have nowhere to turn—no one to talk to."

- "When I feel ashamed, I check out mentally and emotionally. Even with my family."

- "Shame makes you feel estranged from the world. I hide."

- "One time I stopped to get gas and my credit card was declined. The guy gave me a really hard time. As I pulled out of the station, my three-year-old son started crying. I just started screaming, 'Shut up . . . shut up . . . shut up!' I was so ashamed about my card. I went nuts. Then I was ashamed that I yelled at my son."

When it comes to understanding how we defend ourselves against shame, I turn to the wonderful research from the Stone Center at Wellesley. Dr. Linda Hartling, a former relational-cultural theorist at the Stone Center and now the director of Human Dignity and Humiliation Studies, uses the late Karen Horney's work on "moving toward, moving against, and moving away" to outline the strategies of disconnection we use to deal with shame.

According to Dr. Hartling, in order to deal with shame, some of us *move away* by withdrawing, hiding, silencing ourselves, and keeping secrets. Some of us *move toward* by seeking to appease and please. And some of us *move against* by trying to gain power over others, by being aggressive, and by using shame to fight shame (like sending really mean e-mails). Most of us use all of these—at different times with different folks for different reasons. Yet all of these strategies move us away from connection—they are strategies for disconnecting from the pain of shame.

Here's a story about one of my own shame experiences that brings life to all of these concepts. It's not one of my best moments, but it's a good example of why it's important to cultivate and practice shame resilience if we don't want to heap even more shame on top of a painful situation.

First, let me start with a little backstory. Turning down speaking invitations is a vulnerable process for me. Years of pleasing and perfecting have left me feeling less than comfortable with disappointing people—the "good girl" in me hates letting people down. The gremlins whisper, "They'll think you're ungrateful" and "Don't be selfish." I also struggle with the fear that if I say no everyone is going to stop asking. This is when the gremlins say, "You want more time to rest? Be careful what you wish for—this work that you love could all go away."

My new commitment to setting boundaries comes from the twelve years I've spent studying Wholeheartedness and what it takes to make the journey from "What will people think?" to "I am enough." The most connected and compassionate people of those I've interviewed set and respect boundaries. I don't just want to research and travel all of the time talking about being Wholehearted; I want to live it. That means that I turn down about 80 percent of the speaking requests that I receive. I say yes when it works with my family calendar, my research commitments, and my life.

Well, last year I received an e-mail from a man who was really angry with me because I wasn't able to speak at an event that he was hosting. I turned down the invitation because it conflicted with a family birthday. The e-mail was mean-spirited and jam-packed with personal attacks. My gremlins were having a field day!

Rather than replying, I decided to forward it to my husband along with a little note telling him exactly what I thought about this guy and his e-mail. I needed to discharge my shame and anger. Trust me, it was not "good girl" e-mail. I can neither confirm nor deny using the word *horseshit*. Twice.

I hit Reply instead of Forward.

The second my Mac laptop made the airplane swooshing sound that it makes when you hit the Send button, I screamed, "Come back! Please come back!" I was still staring at the screen, totally immobilized by shame layered on shame, when the man fired back a response along the lines of "Aha! I knew it! You *are* a horrible person. You're not Wholehearted. You suck."

The shame attack was already in full swing. My mouth was dry, time was slowing down, and I was seeing tunnel vision. I struggled to swallow as the gremlins started whispering: "You *do* suck!" "How could you be so stupid?" *They always know exactly what to say.* As soon as I could catch my breath, I started murmuring, "Pain, pain, pain, pain, pain . . ."

This strategy is the brainchild of Caroline, a woman whom I interviewed early in my research and then a couple of years later, after she had been practicing shame resilience. Caroline told me that whenever she felt shame, she'd immediately start repeating the word *pain* aloud. "Pain, pain, pain, pain, pain, pain." She told me, "I'm sure it sounds crazy, and I probably look like a nut, but for some reason it really works."

Of course it works! It's a brilliant way to get out of lizard-brain survival mode and pull that prefrontal cortex back online. After one or two minutes of "pain" chanting, I took a deep breath and tried to focus myself. I thought, "Okay. Shame attack. I'm okay. What's next? I can do this."

I recognized the physical symptoms which allowed me to reboot my thinking brain and remember the three ninja-warrior gremlin moves that are the most effective path to shame resilience for me. And fortunately I've been practicing these moves long enough to know that they are totally counterintuitive and I have to trust the process:

1. Practice courage and reach out! Yes, I want to hide, but the way to fight shame and to honor who we are is by sharing our experience with someone who has earned the right to hear it—someone who loves us, not despite our vulnerabilities, but because of them.

2. Talk to myself the way I would talk to someone I really love and whom I'm trying to comfort in the midst of a meltdown: *You're okay. You're human—we all make mistakes. I've got your back.* Normally during a shame attack we talk to ourselves in ways we would NEVER talk to people we love and respect.

3. Own the story! Don't bury it and let it fester or define me. I often say this aloud: *"If you own this story you get to write the ending. If you own this story you get to write the ending."* When we bury the story we forever stay the subject of the story. If we own the story we get to narrate the ending. As Carl Jung said, "I am not what has happened to me. I am what I choose to become."

Even though I knew that the most dangerous thing to do after a shaming experience is to hide or bury our story, I was afraid to make the call. But I did.

I called both my husband, Steve, and my good friend Karen. They gave me what I needed the most: empathy, the best reminder that we're not alone. Rather than judgment (which exacerbates shame), empathy conveys a simple acknowledgment, "You're not alone."

Empathy is connection; it's a ladder out of the shame hole. Not only did Steve and Karen help me climb out by listening and loving me, but they made themselves vulnerable by sharing that they, too, had spent some time in the same hole. Empathy doesn't require that we have the exact same experiences as the person sharing their story with us. Neither Karen nor Steve had sent an e-mail like that, but they were both intimately familiar with the imposter gremlins and the "getting caught" feeling and the "Oh, shit!" experience. Empathy is connecting with the emotion that someone is experiencing, not the event or the circumstance. Shame dissipated the minute I realized that I wasn't alone—that my experience was human.

Interestingly, Steve and Karen's responses were totally different. Steve was more serious and more "Oh, man. I know that feeling!" Karen took an approach that had me laughing in about thirty seconds. What the responses shared in common was the power of "me too." Empathy is a strange and powerful thing. There is no script. There is no right way or wrong way to do it. It's simply listening, holding space, withholding judgment, emotionally connecting, and communicating that incredibly healing message of "You're not alone."

My conversations with Steve and Karen allowed me to move through shame, get back on my emotional feet, and respond to the man's "I knew it!" e-mail from a place of authenticity and self-worth. I owned my part in the angry exchange and apologized for my inappropriate language. I also set clear boundaries around future communications. I never heard from him again.

Shame thrives on secret keeping, and when it comes to secrets, there's some serious science behind the twelve-step program saying, "You're only as sick as your secrets." In a pioneering study, psychologist and University of Texas professor James Pennebaker and his colleagues studied what happened when trauma survivors—specifically rape and incest survivors—kept their experiences secret. The research team found that the act of not discussing a traumatic event or confiding it to another person could be more damaging than the actual event. Conversely, when people shared their stories and experiences, their physical health improved, their doctor's visits decreased, and they showed significant decreases in their stress hormones.

Since his early work on the effects of secret keeping, Pennebaker has focused much of his research on the healing power of expressive writing. In his book *Writing to Heal*, Pennebaker writes, "Since the mid-1980s an increasing number of studies have focused on the value of expressive writing as a way to bring about healing. The evidence is mounting that the act of writing about traumatic experience for as little as fifteen or twenty minutes a day for three or four days can produce measurable changes in physical and mental health. Emotional writing can also affect people's sleep habits, work efficiency, and how they connect with others."

Shame resilience is a practice and like Pennebaker, I think writing about our shame experiences is an incredibly powerful component of the practice. It takes time to cultivate that practice and courage to reach out and talk about hard things. If you're reading this and thinking, *I'd like to be able to have these conversations with my partner or my friend or my child*—do it! If you're reading it and thinking, *Shame has become a management style around here, and it's no wonder that folks are disengaged—we should talk about this*—do it! You don't need to figure it out first or master the information before you engage in conversation. You just have to say, "I've been reading a book and there's a chapter about shame. I'd love to talk about it with you. If I lend you my book, will you take a look?"

The next section is about men, women, shame, and worthiness. I think you'll want to lend them this chapter as well. What I learned about men and shame changed my life.

WEBS AND BOXES: HOW MEN AND WOMEN EXPERIENCE SHAME DIFFERENTLY

For the first four years of my study on shame, I focused solely on women. At that time many researchers believed, and some today still believe, that men and women's experiences of shame are different. I was concerned that if I combined the data from men and women, I'd miss some of the important nuances of their experiences. That I opted to just interview women, I confess, was partially due to my mind-set that when it came to worthiness, women were the ones struggling. At some level, I also think my resistance was based on an intuitive sense that interviewing men would be like stumbling into a new and strange world.

As it turns out, it was definitely a strange new world—a world of unspoken hurt. I got a glimpse into that world in 2005 at the end of one of my lectures. A tall, thin man who I'd guess was in his early sixties followed his wife to the front of the room. He was wearing a yellow Izod golf sweater—an image I'll never forget. I spoke with his wife for a few minutes as I signed a stack of books that she'd bought for herself and her daughters. As she started to walk away, her husband turned to her and said, "I'll be right there—give me a minute."

She clearly didn't want him to stay and talk to me. She tried coaxing him with a couple of "C'mons," but he didn't budge. I, of course, was thinking, *Go with her, dude. You're scaring me.* After a few unsuccessful attempts, she walked toward the back of the room, and he turned to face me at my book-signing table.

It started innocently enough. "I like what you have to say about shame," he told me. "It's interesting."

I thanked him and waited—I could tell there was more coming.

He leaned in closer and asked, "I'm curious. What about men and shame? What have you learned about us?"

I felt instant relief. This wasn't going to take long because I didn't know much. I explained, "I haven't done many interviews with men. I just study women."

He nodded and said, "Well. That's convenient."

I felt the hair on the back of my neck stand up in defense. I forced a smile and asked, "Why convenient?" in the very high voice that I use when I'm uncomfortable. He replied by asking me if I really wanted to know. I told him yes, which was a half-truth. I was on my guard.

Then his eyes welled up with tears. He said, "We have shame. Deep shame. But when we reach out and share our stories, we get the emotional shit beat out of us." I struggled to maintain eye contact with him. His raw pain had touched me, but I was still trying to protect myself. Just as I was about to make a comment about how hard men are on each other, he said, "Before you say anything about those mean coaches, bosses, brothers, and fathers being the only ones . . ." He pointed toward the back of the room where his wife was standing and said, "My wife and daughters—the ones you signed all of those books for—they'd rather see me die on top of my white horse than watch me fall off. You say you want us to be vulnerable and real, but c'mon. You can't stand it. It makes you sick to see us like that."

Holding my breath, I had this very visceral reaction to what he was saying. It hit me the way only truth can. He let out a long sigh, and as quickly as he had begun, he said, "That's all I wanted to say. Thanks for listening." Then he just walked away.

I had spent years researching women and hearing their stories of struggle. In that moment, I realized that men have their own stories and that if we're going to find our way out of shame, it will be together. So, this section is about what I've learned about women, men, how we hurt each other, and how we need each other to heal.

What I've come to believe about men and women now that I've studied both is that men and women are equally affected by shame. The messages and expectations that fuel shame are most definitely organized by gender, but the experience of shame is universal and deeply human.

WOMEN AND THE SHAME WEB

When I asked women to share their definitions or experiences of shame, here's what I heard:

- Look perfect. Do perfect. Be perfect. Anything less than that is shaming.

- Being judged by other mothers.

- Being exposed—the flawed parts of yourself that you want to hide from everyone are revealed.

- No matter what I achieve or how far I've come, where I come from and what I've survived will always keep me from feeling like I'm good enough.

- Even though everyone knows that there's no way to do it all, everyone still expects it. Shame is when you can't pull off looking like it's under control.

- Never enough at home. Never enough at work. Never enough in bed. Never enough with my parents. Shame is never enough.

- No seat at the cool table. The pretty girls are laughing.

If you recall the twelve shame categories (appearance and body image, money and work, motherhood/fatherhood, family, parenting, mental and physical health, addiction, sex, aging, religion, surviving trauma, and being stereotyped or labeled), the primary trigger for women, in terms of its power and universality, is the first one: how we look. Still. After all of the consciousness-raising and critical awareness, we still feel the most shame about not being thin, young, and beautiful enough.

Interestingly, in terms of shame triggers for women, motherhood is a close second. And (bonus!) you don't have to be a mother to experience mother shame. Society views womanhood and motherhood as inextricably bound; therefore our value as women is often determined by where we are in relation to our roles as mothers or potential mothers. Women are constantly asked why they haven't married or, if they're married, why they haven't had children. Even women who are married and have one child are often asked why they haven't had a second child. You've had your kids too far apart? "What were you thinking?" Too close? "Why? That's so unfair to the kids." If you're working outside the home, the first question is "What about the children?" If you're not working, the first question is "What kind of example are you setting for your daughters?" Mother shame is ubiquitous—it's a birthright for girls and women.

But the real struggle for women—what amplifies shame regardless of the category—is that we're expected (and sometimes desire) to be perfect, yet we're not allowed to look as if we're working for it. We want it to just materialize somehow. Everything should be effortless. The expectation is to be natural beauties, natural mothers, natural leaders, and naturally good parents, and we want to belong to naturally fabulous families. Think about how much money has been made selling products that promise "the natural look." And when it comes to work, we love to hear, "She makes it look so easy," or "She's a natural."

As I found myself reading through the pages of definitions and examples provided by women I kept envisioning a web. What I saw was a sticky, complex spiderweb of layered, conflicting, and competing expectations that dictate exactly:

- who we should be

- what we should be

- how we should be

When I think of my own efforts to be everything to everyone—something that women are socialized to do—I can see how every move I make just ensnares me even more. Every effort to twist my way out of the web just leads to becoming more stuck. That's because every choice has consequences or leads to someone being disappointed.

The web is a metaphor for the classic double-bind situation. Writer Marilyn Frye describes a double bind as "a situation in which options are very limited and all of them expose us to penalty, censure, or deprivation." If you take competing and conflicting expectations (which are often unattainable from the get-go) you have this:

- Be perfect, *but* don't make a fuss about it and don't take time away from anything, like your family or your partner or your work, to achieve your perfection. If you're really good, perfection should be easy.

- Don't upset anyone or hurt anyone's feelings, *but* say what's on your mind.

- Dial the sexuality way up (after the kids are down, the dog is walked, and the house is clean), *but* dial it way down at the PTO meeting. And, geez, whatever you do, don't confuse the two—you know how we talk about those PTO sexpots.

- Just be yourself, *but* not if it means being shy or unsure. There's nothing sexier than self-confidence (especially if you're young and smokin' hot).

- Don't make people feel uncomfortable, *but* be honest.

- Don't get too emotional, *but* don't be too detached either. Too emotional and you're hysterical. Too detached and you're a coldhearted bitch.

In a US study on conformity to feminine norms, researchers recently listed the most important attributes associated with "being feminine" as being nice, pursuing a thin body ideal, showing modesty by not calling attention to one's talents or abilities, being domestic, caring for children, investing in a romantic relationship, keeping sexual intimacy contained within one committed relationship, and using our resources to invest in our appearance.

Basically, we have to be willing to stay as small, sweet, and quiet as possible, and use our time and talent to look pretty. Our dreams, ambitions, and gifts are unimportant. God forbid that some young girl who has the cure for cancer tucked away in her abilities finds this list and decides to follow the rules. If she does, we'll never know her genius—and I feel sure of that. Why? Because every successful woman whom I've interviewed has talked to me about the sometimes daily struggle to push past "the rules" so she can assert herself, advocate for her ideas, and feel comfortable with her power and gifts.

Even to me the issue of "stay small, sweet, quiet, and modest" sounds like an outdated problem, but the truth is that women still run into those demands whenever we find and use our voices. When the TEDxHouston video went viral, I wanted to hide. I begged my husband, Steve, to hack into the TED website and "bring the entire thing down!" I fantasized about breaking into the offices where they were keeping the video and stealing it. I was desperate. That was when I realized that I had unconsciously worked throughout my career to keep my work small. I loved writing for my community of readers, because preaching to the choir is easy and relatively safe. The quick and global spread of my work was exactly what I had always tried to avoid. I didn't want the exposure, and I was terrified of the mean-spirited criticism that's so rampant in Internet culture.

Well, the mean-spiritedness happened, and the vast majority of it was directed to reinforcing those norms that we'd love to believe are outdated. When a news outlet shared the video on their site, a heated debate erupted in the comments section of their website about (of course!) my weight. "How can she talk about worthiness when she clearly needs to lose fifteen pounds?" On another site, a debate grew about the appropriateness of mothers having breakdowns. "I feel sorry for her children. Good mothers don't fall apart." Another commenter wrote, "Less research. More Botox."

Something similar happened when I wrote an article on imperfection for CNN.com. To accompany the article, the editor used a photo I had taken of a good friend who had "I am Enough" written across the top of her chest. It's a beautiful photo that I have hanging in my study as a reminder. Well, that fueled comments like "She may believe that she's enough, but by the look of that chest, she could use some more," and "If I looked like Brené Brown, I'd embrace imperfection too."

I know that these examples are symptomatic of the cruelty culture that we live in today and that everyone is fair game, but think about how and what they chose to attack. They went after my appearance and my mothering—two kill shots taken straight from the list of feminine norms. They didn't go after my intellect or my arguments. That wouldn't hurt enough.

So, no, those societal norms aren't outdated, even if they're reductionist and squeeze the life out of us, and shame is the route to enforcing them. Which is another reminder of why shame resilience is a prerequisite for vulnerability. I believe I dared greatly in my TEDxHouston talk. Talking about my struggles was a courageous thing for me to do, given my drive to self-protect and use research as armor. And the only reason I'm still standing (and sitting here writing this book) is because I've cultivated some pretty fierce shame resilience skills and I'm crystal clear that courage is an important value to me.

I clearly saw that these comments triggered shame in me and I could quickly reality-check the messages. Yes, they still hurt. Yes, I was pissed. Yes, I cried my eyes out. Yes, I wanted to disappear. But I gave myself permission to feel these things for a couple of hours or days, then I reached out, talked through my feelings with people I trust and love, and I moved on. I felt more courageous, more compassionate, more connected. (*I also stopped reading anonymous comments. If you're not in the arena with the rest of us, fighting and getting your ass kicked on occasion, I'm not interested in your feedback.*)

HOW MEN EXPERIENCE SHAME

When I asked men to define shame or give me an answer, here's what I heard:

- Shame is failure. At work. On the football field. In your marriage. In bed. With money. With your children. It doesn't matter—shame is failure.

- Shame is being wrong. Not doing it wrong, but being wrong.

- Shame is a sense of being defective.

- Shame happens when people think you're soft. It's degrading and shaming to be seen as anything but tough.

- Revealing any weakness is shaming. Basically, shame is weakness.

- Showing fear is shameful. You can't show fear. You can't be afraid—no matter what.

- Shame is being seen as "the guy you can shove up against the lockers."

- Our worst fear is being criticized or ridiculed— either one of these is extremely shaming.

Basically, men live under the pressure of one unrelenting message: Do not be perceived as weak.

Whenever my graduate students were going to do interviews with men, I told them to prepare for three things: high school stories, sports metaphors, and the word *pussy*. If you're thinking that you can't believe I just wrote that, I get it. It's one of my least favorite words. But as a researcher, I know it's important to be honest about what emerged, and that word came up all of the time in the interviews. It didn't matter if the man was eighteen or eighty, if I asked, "What's the shame message?" the answer was "Don't be a pussy."

When I first started writing about my work with men, I used the image of a box—something that looked like a shipping crate—to explain how shame traps men. Like the demands on women to be naturally beautiful, thin, and perfect at everything, especially motherhood, the box has rules that tell men what they should and shouldn't do, and who they're allowed to be. But for men, every rule comes back to the same mandate: "Don't be weak."

I'll never forget when a twenty-year-old man who was part of a small group of college students that I was interviewing said, "Let me show you the box." I knew he was a tall guy, but when he stood up, it was clear that he was at least six foot four. He said, "Imagine living like this," as he crouched down and pretended that he was stuffed inside a small box.

Still hunched over, he said, "You really only have three choices. You spend your life fighting to get out, throwing punches at the side of the box and hoping it will break. You always feel angry and you're always swinging. Or you just give up. You don't give a shit about anything." At that point he slumped over on the ground. You could have heard a pin drop in the room.

Then he stood up, shook his head, and said, "Or you stay high so you don't really notice how unbearable it is. That's the easiest way." The students grabbed on to *stay high* like a life preserver and broke into nervous laughter. This happens a lot when you're talking about shame or vulnerability—anything to cut the tension.

But this brave young man wasn't laughing and neither was I. His demonstration was one of the most honest and courageous things I've ever had the privilege of seeing, and I know that the people in that room were deeply affected by it. After the group interview, he told me about his experiences growing up. He had been a passionate artist as a child, and he winced as he described how he was sure from an early age that he'd be happy if he could spend his life painting and drawing.

He said that one day he was in the kitchen with his dad and uncle. His uncle pointed to a collection of his art that was plastered on the refrigerator and said jokingly to his father, "What? You're raising a faggot artist now?"

After that, he said, his father, who had always been neutral about his art, forbade him from taking classes. Even his mother, who had always been so proud of his talent, agreed that it was "a little too girly." He told me that he'd drawn a picture of his house the day before all of this happened, and to that day it was the last thing he'd ever drawn. That night I wept for him and for all of us who never got to see his work. I think about him all of the time and hope he has reconnected with his art. I know it's a tremendous loss for him, and I'm equally positive that the world is missing out.

PAY NO ATTENTION TO THAT MAN BEHIND THE CURTAIN

As I've learned more about men and their experiences with shame, I still see that image of a shipping crate with a big stamp across it that reads, "CAUTION: Do Not Be Perceived as Weak." I see how boys are issued a crate when they're born. It's not too crowded when they're toddlers. They're still small and can move around a bit. They can cry and hold on to mamma, but as they grow older, there's less and less wiggle room. By the time they're grown men, it's suffocating.

But just as with women, men are caught in their own double bind. Over the past couple of years, especially since the economic downturn, what I have started to see is the box from *The Wizard of Oz*. I'm talking about the small, curtain-concealed box that the wizard stands in as he's controlling his mechanical "great and powerful" Oz image. As scarcity has grabbed hold of our culture, it's not just "Don't be perceived as weak," but also "You better be great and all powerful." This image first came to mind when I interviewed a man who was in deep shame about getting "downsized." He told me, "It's funny. My father knows. My two closest friends know. But my wife doesn't know. It's been six months, and every morning I still get dressed and leave the house like I'm going to work. I drive across town, sit in coffee shops, and look for a job."

I'm a skilled interviewer, but I can imagine that the look on my face conveyed something like "How on earth did you pull that off?" Without waiting for my next question, he answered, "She doesn't want to know. If she already knows, she wants me to keep pretending. Trust me, if I find another job and tell her after I'm back at work, she'll be grateful. Knowing would change the way she feels about me. She didn't sign up for this."

I was not prepared to hear over and over from men how the women—the mothers, sisters, girlfriends, wives—in their lives are constantly criticizing them for not being open and vulnerable and intimate, all the while they are standing in front of that cramped wizard closet where their men are huddled inside, adjusting the curtain and making sure *no one sees in and no one gets out*. There was a moment when I was driving home from an interview with a small group of men and thought, *Holy shit. I am the patriarchy.*

Here's the painful pattern that emerged from my research with men: We ask them to be vulnerable, we beg them to let us in, and we plead with them to tell us when they're afraid, but the truth is that most women can't stomach it. In those moments when real vulnerability happens in men, most of us recoil with fear and that fear manifests as everything from disappointment to disgust. And men are very smart. They know the risks, and they see the look in our eyes when we're thinking, *C'mon! Pull it together. Man up.* As Joe Reynolds, one of my mentors and the dean at our church, once told me during a conversation about men, shame, and vulnerability, "Men know what women really want. They want us to pretend to be vulnerable. We get really good at pretending."

Covert shame hurts just as much as overt shame. Take, for example, the man who told me that he was always feeling shame with his wife around money. He said the latest instance was when his wife came home and said, "I just saw Katie's new house! It's amazing. She's so happy to finally get that dream house. On top of that, she's going to quit working next year."

He told me his immediate response was rage. So he picked a fight with his wife about her mother coming to visit, and then quickly disappeared to another part of the house. As we were talking about this conversation, he said, "It was shame. Why did she have to say that? I get it. Katie's husband makes a lot of money. He takes better care of her. I can't compete."

When I asked him if he thought that it was her intention to hurt him or shame him, he responded, "I'm not sure. Who knows? I turned down a job that paid a lot more but required traveling three weeks out of the month. She said she was supportive, and that she and the kids would miss me too much, but now she makes little comments about money all of the time. I have no idea what to think."

PISSED OFF OR SHUT DOWN

I don't want to oversimplify something as complex as the response to shame, but I have to say that when it comes to men, there seem to be two primary responses: pissed off or shut down. Of course, like women, as men develop shame resilience, this changes, and men learn to respond to shame with awareness, self-compassion, and empathy. But without that awareness, when men feel that rush of inadequacy and smallness, they normally respond with anger and/or by completely turning off.

Once I had collected enough interviews to start seeing strong patterns and themes, I scheduled interviews with several male therapists who specialize in men's issues. I wanted to make sure that I wasn't filtering what I heard from the men through my own experiences. When I asked one of these therapists about the concept of "pissed off or shut down," he told me this story to illustrate the point.

When he was a freshman in high school, he tried out and made the football team. On the first day of practice, his coach told the boys to line up on the line of scrimmage. The therapist had grown up playing a lot of football in his neighborhood, but this was his first experience on a field, in full pads, across from boys whose goal was to flatten him. He said, "I was suddenly afraid. I was thinking about how much it was going to hurt, and I guess that fear showed up on my face."

He said his coach yelled his last name and said, "Don't be a pussy! Get on the line." He said he immediately felt shame coursing through his body. "In that single moment, I became very clear about how the world works and what it means to be a man:

"I am not allowed to be afraid.

"I am not allowed to show fear.

"I am not allowed to be vulnerable.

"Shame is being afraid, showing fear, or being vulnerable."

When I asked him what he did next, he looked me in the eye and said, "I turned my fear into rage and steamrolled over the guy in front of me. It worked so well that I spent the next twenty years turning my fear and vulnerability into rage and steamrolling anyone who was across from me. My wife. My children. My employees. There was no other way out from underneath the fear and shame."

I heard such grief and clarity in his voice as he was saying this to me. It made total sense. Fear and vulnerability are powerful emotions. You can't just wish them away. You have to do something with them. Many men, in fact, use very physiological descriptions when they talk to me about "pissed off or shut down." It's almost as if shame, criticism, and ridicule are physically intolerable.

The therapist concluded, "I got into therapy when my rage and my drinking were no longer manageable. When it started costing me my marriage and my relationships with my children. That's why I do the work I do today."

Shame resilience—the four elements we discussed in the previous chapter—is about finding a middle path, an option that allows us to stay engaged and to find the emotional courage we need to respond in a way that aligns with our values.

I'M ONLY AS HARD ON OTHERS AS I AM ON MYSELF

Just like the father coming down on his budding artist son or the coach giving his player a hard time, women can also be very hard on other women. We are hard on others because we're hard on ourselves. That's exactly how judgment works. Finding someone to put down, judge, or criticize becomes a way to get out of the web or call attention away from our box. If you're doing worse than I am at something, I think, my chances of surviving are better.

Steve and I met lifeguarding and coaching swimming. The big rule in lifeguarding is to utilize any means possible before you actually jump in and try to pull someone out of the water. Even though you're a strong swimmer and the person you're trying to help is half your size, a desperate person will do anything to save themselves—to grab a breath—including drowning you in their effort to survive. The same is true for women and the shame web. We're so desperate to get out and stay out of shame that we're constantly serving up the people around us as more deserving prey.

What's ironic (or perhaps natural) is that research tells us that we judge people in areas where we're vulnerable to shame, especially picking folks who are doing worse than we're doing. If I feel good about my parenting, I have no interest in judging other people's choices. If I feel good about my body, I don't go around making fun of other people's weight or appearance. We're hard on each other because we're using each other as a launching pad out of our own perceived shaming deficiency. It's hurtful and ineffective, and if you look at the mean-girl culture in middle schools and high schools, it's also contagious. We've handed this counterfeit survival mechanism down to our children.

In my interviews with teachers and school administrators, two patterns emerged that speak directly to this issue. The first pattern reported by faculty and principals was that often the children who are engaging in the bullying behaviors or vying for social ranking by putting down others have parents who engage in the same behaviors. When it came to girls, the phrase that kept emerging from the interviews was "The parents aren't upset by their daughters' behaviors; they're proud of them for being popular." One school administrator likened this behavior to the fathers who first ask, "Well, did he at least win the fight?"

The other pattern, which has only emerged in the last

couple of years, is the age of the children when this starts happening. When I started this work, bullying wasn't a hot topic, but as a shame researcher, I was aware that it was a growing trend. In fact, I wrote an op-ed on bullying and reality television for the *Houston Chronicle* over ten years ago. Back then my focus was teenagers because the data pointed to adolescence as the prime age range for these behaviors. In the past couple of years, I'm hearing about girls and boys as young as first grade engaging in these behaviors.

How do we break this insidious pattern? Maybe by deciding (and showing our children) that the solution to being stuck in shame is not to denigrate others stuck just like us, but to join hands and pull free together. For example, if we're at the grocery store, and we push our cart past another mother whose child is screaming bloody murder and throwing Cheerios on the floor, we have a choice. If we choose to use the moment to confirm that we're better than she is, and that she's stuck in the web in ways we are not, we will roll our eyes in disapproval and walk by. Our other choice, though, is to flash that mother our best "you're not alone—I've been there, sister" smile because we know what she's feeling. Yes, empathy requires some vulnerability, and we risk getting back a "mind your own damn business" look, but it's worth it. It doesn't just loosen up the web for her. It loosens it up for us the next time it's our child and our Cheerios—and you can bet it will be.

What gives me hope about our willingness to extend a hand back and support each other is the increasing number of men and women I encounter who are willing to risk vulnerability and share their stories of shame resilience. I see this in formal and informal mentoring programs. I see this from folks who are writing blogs and sharing their experiences with readers. I see it in schools and programs that not only are becoming increasingly less tolerant of student bullying but are holding teachers, administrators, and parents accountable for their behaviors. Adults are being asked to model the Wholeheartedness that they want to see in the children.

There is a quiet transformation happening that is moving us from "turning on each other" to "turning toward each other." Without question, that transformation will require shame resilience. If we're willing to dare greatly and risk vulnerability with each other, worthiness has the power to set us free.

IT'S NOT ABOUT THE BACK FAT:
MEN, WOMEN, SEX, AND BODY IMAGE

In 2006 I met with twenty-two community college students, male and female, to talk about shame. It was my first coed large group interview. At some point, a young man in his early twenties explained how he had recently divorced his wife after coming back from serving in the military and finding out that she was having an affair. He said he wasn't surprised because he never felt "good enough for her." He explained that he constantly asked her what she needed and wanted, and that every time he got close to meeting her needs, she "moved the goalpost another ten feet."

A young woman in the class spoke up and said, "Guys are the same way. They're never satisfied either. We're never pretty, sexy, or skinny enough." Within seconds a conversation broke out about body image and sex. The discussion was mostly about how it's so scary to have sex with someone you care about when you're worried about how your body looks. The young women who started the conversation said, "It's not easy to have sex and keep your stomach sucked in. How can we get into it when we're worried about our back fat?"

The young man who had shared the story of his divorce slammed his hand down on his desk and shouted, "It's not about the back fat! You're worried about it. We're not. We don't give a shit!" The class fell completely quiet. He took a couple of deep breaths and said, "Stop making up all of this stuff about what we're thinking! What we're really thinking is 'Do you love me? Do you care about me? Do you want me? Am I important to you? Am I good enough?' That's what we're thinking. When it comes to sex, it feels like our life is on the line, and you're worried about that crap?"

At that point, half of the young men in the room were so emotional that they had their faces in their hands. A few girls were in tears, and I couldn't breathe. The young woman who had brought up the body image issue said, "I don't understand. My last boyfriend was always criticizing my body."

The young vet who had just brought us all to our knees replied, "That's because he's an asshole. It's not because he's a guy. Some of us are just guys. Give us a break. Please."

A middle-aged man in the group joined in, staring straight down at his desk. "It's true. When you want to be with us . . . in that way . . . it makes us feel more worthy. We stand a little taller. Believe in ourselves more. I don't know why, but it's true. And I've been married since I was eighteen. It still feels that way with my wife."

Never in my life before that moment did I think about men feeling vulnerable about sex. Never did I consider that their self-worth was in any way on the line. I didn't understand. So I interviewed many more men about the topic of sexuality, shame, and worthiness, including mental health professionals. In one of my final interviews on the topic, I sat down with a therapist who had spent more than twenty-five years working with men. He explained that from the time boys are eight to ten years old, they learn that initiating sex is their responsibility and that sexual rejection soon becomes the hallmark of masculine shame.

He explained, "Even in my own life, when my wife isn't interested, I still have to battle feelings of shame. It doesn't matter if I intellectually understand why she's not in the mood. I'm vulnerable and it's very difficult." When I asked him about his work around addiction and pornography, he gave me an answer that helped me understand that issue in an entirely new light. He said, "For five bucks and five minutes, you think you're getting what you need, and you don't have to risk rejection."

The reason that response was so revelatory to me was because it was so utterly different from what women felt. After interviewing women for a decade, it was clear that women see the issue of men and pornography as having to do with their own inadequate appearance and/or their lack of sexual expertise. At the end of my interview with this wonderful and wise man, he said, "I guess the secret is that sex is terrifying for most men. That's why you see everything from porn to the violent, desperate attempts to exercise power and control. Rejection is deeply painful."

Cultivating intimacy—physical or emotional—is almost impossible when our shame triggers meet head-on and create the perfect shame storm. Sometimes these shame storms are directly about sex and intimacy, but often there are outlying gremlins wreaking havoc in our relationships. Common issues include body image, aging, appearance, money, parenting, motherhood, exhaustion, resentment, and fear. When I asked men, women, and couples how they practiced Wholeheartedness around these very sensitive and personal issues, one answer came up again and again: honest, loving conversations that require major vulnerability. We have to be able to talk about how we feel, what we need and desire, and we have to be able to listen with an open heart and an open mind. There is no intimacy without vulnerability. Yet another powerful example of vulnerability as courage.

THE WORDS WE CAN NEVER TAKE BACK

Too close for missiles, I'm switching to guns.

—*Top Gun*

When I talk to couples, I can see how shame creates one of the dynamics most lethal to a relationship. Women, who feel shame when they don't feel heard or validated, often resort to pushing and provoking with criticism ("Why don't you ever do enough?" or "You never get it right"). Men, in turn, who feel shame when they feel criticized for being inadequate, either shut down (leading women to poke and provoke more) or come back with anger.

For the first few years of our marriage, Steve and I fell into this pattern. I remember one argument when we were both angry beyond belief. After ten minutes of endless chiding on my part, he turned to me and said, "Leave me alone for twenty minutes. I'm done. I won't do this anymore." When he shut and locked the door, I got so mad that I actually banged on the door and said, "Get back out here and fight with me." In that moment, when I heard myself, I saw what was happening. He was on the verge of shutting down or raging, and I was feeling unheard and misunderstood. The result was mutual desperation.

Steve and I are heading into our eighteenth year of marriage, and this year we'll celebrate the twenty-fifth anniversary of our first date. He is, without question, the best thing that's ever happened to me. When we got married, neither one of us had any idea what a good partnership looked like or what it took to make it work. If you asked us today what we believe is the key to our relationship, the answer would be vulnerability, love, humor, respect, shame-free fighting, and blame-free living. We learned some of that on our own through good ol' trial and error, but we also learned from my work and the research participants who were brave enough to share their stories with me. I'm so grateful to them.

I think we can all agree that feeling shame is an incredibly painful experience. What we often don't realize is that perpetrating shame is equally as painful, and no one does that with the precision of a partner or a parent. These are the people who know us the best and who bear witness to our vulnerabilities and fears. Thankfully, we can apologize for shaming someone we love, but the truth is that those shaming comments leave marks. And shaming someone we love around vulnerability is the most serious of all security breaches. Even if we apologize, we've done serious damage because we've demonstrated our willingness to use sacred information as a weapon.

In *The Gifts of Imperfection*, I share the definition of love that I developed based on my data. Here it is:

> We cultivate love when we allow our most vulnerable and powerful selves to be deeply seen and known, and when we honor the spiritual connection that grows from that offering with trust, respect, kindness, and affection.
>
> Love is not something we give or get; it is

something that we nurture and grow, a connection that can only be cultivated between two people when it exists within each one of them—we can only love others as much as we love ourselves.

Shame, blame, disrespect, betrayal, and the withholding of affection damage the roots from which love grows. Love can only survive these injuries if they are acknowledged, healed, and rare.

Developing this definition was one of the hardest things I've ever done. Professionally, it just seemed arrogant to try to define something as big and important as love. It felt like an endeavor best left to the poets and artists. My motivation was not to "nail it," but to start a conversation about what we need and want from love. I don't care if I'm wrong, but let's talk about love. Let's have some conversations about the experience that gives meaning to our lives.

Personally, I fought the data with everything I have. Over and over, I heard the idea of self-love as a prerequisite to loving others, and I hated it. Sometimes it's so much easier to love Steve and the kids than it is to love myself. It's so much easier to accept their quirks and eccentricities than it is to practice self-love around what I see as my deep flaws. But in practicing self-love over the past couple of years, I can say that it has immeasurably deepened my relationships with the people I love. It's given me the courage to show up and be vulnerable in new ways, and that's what love is all about.

As we think about shame and love, the most pressing question is this: Are we practicing love? Yes, most of us are really good at professing it—sometimes ten times a day. But are we walking the talk? Are we being our most vulnerable selves? Are we showing trust, kindness, affection, and respect to our partners? It's not the lack of professing that gets us in trouble in our relationships; it's failing to practice love that leads to hurt.

BECOMING REAL

Do you remember how I mentioned earlier in the chapter that researchers found that attributes such as nice, thin, and modest were qualities that our culture associates with femininity? Well, when looking at the attributes associated with masculinity in the US, the same researchers identified the following: winning, emotional control, risk-taking, violence, dominance, playboy, self-reliance, primacy of work, power over women, disdain for homosexuality, and pursuit of status.

Understanding these lists and what they mean is critically important to understanding shame and cultivating resilience. As I explained in the beginning of the chapter, shame is universal, but the messages and expectations that drive shame are organized by gender. These feminine and masculine norms are the foundation of shame triggers, and here's why: If women want to play by the rules, they need to be sweet, thin, and pretty, stay quiet, be perfect moms and wives, and not own their power. One move outside of these expectations and BAM! The shame web closes in. Men, on the other hand, need to stop feeling, start earning, put everyone in their place, and climb their way to the top or die trying. Push open the lid of your box to grab a breath of air, or slide that curtain back a bit to see what's going on, and BAM! Shame cuts you down to size.

I think it's important to add that for men there's also a cultural message that promotes homophobic cruelty. If you want to be masculine in our culture, it's not enough to be straight— you must also show an outward disgust toward the gay community. The idea of "*do this* or *dislike these people* if you want to be accepted into our group" emerged as a major shame setup in the research.

It doesn't matter if the group is a church or a gang or a sewing circle or masculinity itself, asking members to dislike, disown, or distance themselves from another group of people as a condition of "belonging" is always about control and power. I think we have to question the intentions of any group that insists on disdain toward other people as a membership requirement. It may be disguised as belonging, but real belonging doesn't necessitate disdain.

When I look at those eleven attributes of masculinity, that's not the kind of man I want to spend my life with and that's not how I want to raise my son. The word that comes to my mind when I think about a life built around those qualities is *lonely*. The picture in my mind goes back to the Wizard of Oz. He's not a real person with human needs, but a "great and powerful" projection of what a man is supposed to be. Lonely, exhausting, and soul-sucking.

When I talk to men and women with high levels of shame resilience, they are keenly aware of these lists. They keep those strictures in mind so that when shame starts creeping up on them, or they find themselves fully in shame, they can reality-check these "norms," thus practicing the second element of shame resilience—critical awareness. Basically, they can choose consciously not to play along.

The man in shame says, "I'm not supposed to get emotional when I have to lay off these people."

The man practicing shame resilience responds, "I'm not buying into this message. I've worked with these guys for five years. I know their families. I'm allowed to care about them."

Shame whispers in the ear of the woman who's out of town on business, "You're not a good mother because you're going to miss your son's class play."

She replies, "I hear you, but I'm not playing that tape today. My mothering is way bigger than one class performance. You can leave now."

One of the most powerful ways that our shame triggers get reinforced is when we enter into a social contract based on these gender straitjackets. Our relationships are defined by women and men saying, "I'll play my role, and you play yours." One of the patterns revealed in the research was how all that role playing becomes almost unbearable around midlife. Men feel increasingly disconnected, and the fear of failure becomes paralyzing. Women are exhausted, and for the first time they begin to clearly see that the expectations are impossible. The accomplishments, accolades, and acquisitions that are a seductive part of living by this contract start to feel like a Faustian bargain.

Remembering that shame is the fear of disconnection—the fear that we're unlovable and don't belong—makes it easy to see why so many people in midlife overfocus on their children's lives, work sixty hours a week, or turn to affairs, addiction, and disengagement. We start to unravel. The expectations and messages that fuel shame keep us from fully realizing who we are as people.

Today, I look back and feel so grateful to women and men who have shared their stories with me. I'm thankful for the people who were brave enough to say, "These are my secrets and my fears, here's how they brought me to my knees, and here's how I learned to stand in my worthiness again." I'm also indebted to the man in the yellow Izod sweater. His vulnerability and honesty set in motion work that has forever changed my career and, more importantly, my life.

As I look back on what I've learned about shame, gender, and worthiness, the greatest lesson is this: If we're going to find our way out of shame and back to each other, vulnerability is the path and courage is the light. To set down those lists of what *we're supposed to be* is brave. To love ourselves and support each other in the process of becoming real is perhaps the greatest single act of daring greatly.

I'll leave you with this passage from the 1922 children's classic *The Velveteen Rabbit* by Margery Williams. My friend DeeDee Parker Wright sent it to me last year with a note that said, "This is what being Wholehearted is all about." I agree. It's a beautiful reminder of how much easier it is to become real when we know we're loved:

> "Real isn't how you are made," said the Skin Horse. "It's a thing that happens to you. When a child loves you for a long, long time, not just to play with, but really loves you, then you become Real."
>
> "Does it hurt?" asked the Rabbit.
>
> "Sometimes," said the Skin Horse, for he was always truthful. "When you are Real, you don't mind being hurt."
>
> "Does it happen all at once, like being wound up," he asked, "or bit by bit?"
>
> "It doesn't happen all at once," said the Skin Horse. "You become. It takes a long time. That's why it doesn't often happen to people who break easily, or have sharp edges, or who

have to be carefully kept. Generally, by the time you are Real, most of your hair has been loved off, and your eyes drop out, and you get loose in the joints and very shabby. But these things don't matter at all, because once you are Real, you can't be ugly, except to people who don't understand."

CHAPTER 4
THE VULNERABILITY
ARMORY

As children we found ways to protect ourselves from vulnerability, from being hurt, diminished, and disappointed. We put on armor; we used our thoughts, emotions, and behaviors as weapons; and we learned how to make ourselves scarce, even to disappear. Now as adults we realize that to live with courage, purpose, and connection—to be the person whom we long to be—we must again be vulnerable. We must take off the armor, put down the weapons, show up, and let ourselves be seen.

THE word *persona* is the Greek term for "stage mask." In my work masks and armor are perfect metaphors for how we protect ourselves from the discomfort of vulnerability. Masks make us feel safer even when they become suffocating. Armor makes us feel stronger even when we grow weary from dragging the extra weight around. The irony is that when we're standing across from someone who is hidden or shielded by masks and armor, we feel frustrated and disconnected. That's the paradox here: *Vulnerability is the last thing I want you to see in me, but the first thing I look for in you.*

If I were directing a play about the vulnerability armory, the setting would be a middle school cafeteria and the characters would be our eleven-, twelve-, and thirteen-year-old selves. I pick this age because armor can be hard to see on adults. Once we've worn it long enough, it molds to our shape and is ultimately undetectable—it's like a second skin. Masks are the same way. I've interviewed hundreds of participants who have conveyed the same fear: "I can't take the mask off now—no one knows what I really look like. Not my partner, not my kids, not my friends. They've never met the real me. I'm not even sure who I am under here."

Preteens or tweens, though, are much different. Upper elementary school and middle school was where most of us started to try on new and different forms of protection. At this tender age, the armor is still awkward and ill fitting. Kids are clumsy in their efforts to hide fear and self-doubt, which makes it easier for observers to see exactly what armor they are using and why. And depending on the level of shame and fear, most kids have yet to be convinced that the heaviness of the armor or the suffocating nature of a mask is worth the effort. They put on and take off personas and protection without hesitation, sometimes in the same sentence: "I don't care what those people think. They're so stupid. The dance is stupid. Can you call their moms and find out what they're wearing? I hope I get to dance."

The after-school specials of my youth seemed to be dedicated to exploring just these ideas. They brought us the mean boy who really just wanted to be included and the know-it-all girl who was showing off at school to hide her misery over her parents' recent divorce. Our protection mechanisms may be more sophisticated now that we're adults, but most of us learned about armor during these raw and impressionable years, and most of us can be brought back to that place in a heartbeat.

From my personal experiences, I can tell you that the most difficult thing about parenting a daughter in middle school is coming face-to-face with the awkward, sweaty-palmed seventh-grader who lives inside me. My instinct back then was to duck and run, and I often feel that impulse creeping up on me when Ellen is in a struggle. I swear there are times when she's describing a situation at school that I can actually smell my middle school cafeteria.

Whether we're fourteen or fifty-four, our armor and our

masks are as individualized and unique as the personal vulnerability, discomfort, and pain we're trying to minimize. That's why I was surprised to discover that we all share a small array of common protection mechanisms. Our armor may be custom-made, but certain parts of it are interchangeable. By prying open the doors of the armory, we can expose to daylight the more universal bits and pieces and also rummage through the closets that house less universal, but often dangerous, items of vulnerability protection.

If you're like me, it's tempting to take this information and create your own after-school special. As these shared mechanisms started to emerge from the data, my first instinct was to label behavior and cast the people around me as stereotypes: "She so wears this mask, and my neighbor totally uses this armor." It's human nature to want to categorize and oversimplify, but I think this misses the point. None of us uses just one of these shared defenses. Most of us will be able to relate to almost all of them, depending on the different circumstances we navigate. My hope is that a peek inside the armory will help us to look inside ourselves. How do we protect ourselves? When and how did we start using these defense mechanisms? What would it take to make us put the armor away?

THE "ENOUGH" MANDATE

For me the most powerful part of this research was discovering the strategies that seem to empower people to take off the masks and armor that I'm about to describe. I assumed that I'd find unique strategies for each protection mechanism, similar to what emerged in the ten guideposts I write about in *The Gifts of Imperfection*. But that wasn't the case here.

In the first chapter, I talked about "enough" as the opposite of scarcity, and the properties of scarcity as shame, comparison, and disengagement. Well, it appears that believing that we're "enough" is the way out of the armor—it gives us permission to take off the mask. With that sense of "enough" comes an embrace of worthiness, boundaries, and engagement. This lay at the core of every strategy illuminated by the research participants for freeing themselves from their armor:

- I am enough (worthiness versus shame).

- I've had enough (boundaries versus one-uping and comparison).

- Showing up, taking risks, and letting myself be seen is enough (engagement versus disengagement).

As you read through this chapter, I think it's helpful for you to know that every single person I interviewed spoke about struggling with vulnerability. It's not as if there are lucky people among us who can openly embrace vulnerability without reservation, hesitation, or fear. When it comes to uncertainty, risk, and emotional exposure, what I heard over and over were descriptions of people trying on some kind of armor before finally letting it go:

- "My first instinct is to _____, but that never worked, so now I _____, and that's changed my life."

- "I spent years _____ until one day I tried _____, and it made my marriage stronger."

Last year I gave a talk on vulnerability to 350 SWAT team officers, parole officers, and jailers. (Yes, it was as intimidating as it sounds.) A SWAT officer walked up to me after the talk and said, "The only reason we listened to you is because you're just as bad at being open as we are. If you didn't wrestle with being vulnerable, we wouldn't trust you one bit."

Not only did I believe him, but I totally agreed. I trust the strategies that I'm writing about here for two reasons. First, the research participants who shared them with me had wrestled with the same gremlins, discomfort, and self-doubt that we all face. Second, I've practiced these strategies in my own life and know for a fact that they aren't just game changers—they're lifesavers.

The three forms of shielding that I am about to introduce are what I refer to as the "common vulnerability arsenal" because I have found that we all incorporate them into our personal armor in some way. These include **foreboding joy**, or the paradoxical dread that clamps down on momentary joyfulness; **perfectionism**, or believing that doing everything perfectly means you'll never feel shame; and **numbing**, the embrace of whatever deadens the pain of discomfort and pain. Each shield is followed by "Daring Greatly" strategies, all variants on "being enough" that have proved to be effective at disarming the three common forms of shielding.

THE COMMON VULNERABILITY SHIELDS
THE SHIELD: FOREBODING JOY

Given that I study emotions like shame, fear, and vulnerability, I hardly expected to one day be telling you that exploring the construct of joy turned my professional and personal life upside down. But it's true. In fact, having spent several years studying what it means to feel joyful, I'd argue that joy is probably the most difficult emotion to really feel. Why? Because when we lose the ability or willingness to be vulnerable, joy becomes something we approach with deep foreboding. This shift from our younger self's greeting of joy with unalloyed delight happens slowly and outside of our awareness. We don't seem to even know that it's happening or why. We just know that we crave more joy in our lives, that we are joy starved.

In a culture of deep scarcity—of never feeling safe, certain, and sure enough—joy can feel like a setup. We wake up in the morning and think, *Work is going well. Everyone in the family is healthy. No major crises are happening. The house is still standing. I'm working out and feeling good. Oh, shit. This is bad. This is really bad. Disaster must be lurking right around the corner.*

Or we get promoted, and our first thought is *Too good to be true. What's the catch?* We find out we're pregnant, and we think, *Our daughter is healthy and happy, so something really bad is going to happen with this baby. I just know it.* We're taking our first family vacation, but rather than being excited, we're making plans for the plane to go down or the ship to sink.

We're always waiting for the other shoe to drop. That expression originated in the early 1900s, when new immigrants and people flooding to the cities were crammed into tenement housing where you could literally hear your upstairs neighbor taking off his shoes at night. Once you heard the first shoe hit the floor you *waited for the other shoe to drop.* Even though the world today is much safer in many ways than it was in the early part of that century, and our life expectancy is far greater than that of the folks who were listening for a second shoe to hit the floor, the stakes feel so much higher to us. Most of us today think of the other shoe as something terrifying: a terrorist attack, a natural disaster, an *E. coli* outbreak in our local grocery store, a school shooting.

When I started asking participants about the experiences that left them feeling the most vulnerable, I didn't expect joy to be one of the answers. I expected fear and shame, but not the joyful moments of their lives. I was shocked to hear people say they were at their most vulnerable when:

- Standing over my children while they're sleeping

- Acknowledging how much I love my husband/wife

- Knowing how good I've got it

- Loving my job

- Spending time with my parents

- Watching my parents with my children

- Thinking about my relationship with my boyfriend

- Getting engaged

- Going into remission

- Having a baby

- Getting promoted

- Being happy

- Falling in love

Not only was I shocked to hear these answers, I knew I was in trouble.

Before my 2007 ~~breakdown~~ spiritual awakening, foreboding joy was one of my own unconscious pieces of armor. When I first made the connection between vulnerability and joy reported by participants, I could barely breathe. I had considered my constant disaster planning as my little secret. I was convinced that I was the only one who stood over my children while they slept and, in the split second that I became engulfed with love and adoration, pictured something really terrible happening to them. I was sure that no one but me pictured car wrecks and rehearsed the horrific phone conversations with the police that all of us dread.

One of the first stories I heard was from a woman in her late forties. "I used to take every good thing and imagine the worst possible disaster," she told me. "I would literally picture the worst-case scenario and try to control all of the outcomes. When my daughter got into the college of her dreams, I just knew something bad would happen if she moved too far away. I spent the entire summer before she left trying to convince her to go to a local school. It crushed her confidence and took the fun out of our last summer. It was a painful lesson. Now I cross my fingers, stay grateful, pray, and try like hell to push the bad images out of my head. Unfortunately, I've passed that way of thinking down to my daughter. She's increasingly afraid to try new things, especially when her life is going well. She says she doesn't want to 'tempt fate.'"

A man in his early sixties told me, "I used to think the best way to go through life was to expect the worst. That way, if it happened, you were prepared, and if it didn't happen, you were pleasantly surprised. Then I was in a car accident and my wife was killed. Needless to say, expecting the worst didn't prepare me at all. And worse, I still grieve for all of those wonderful moments we shared and that I didn't fully enjoy. My commitment to her is to fully enjoy every moment now. I just wish she was here, now that I know how to do that."

These stories illustrate how the concept of foreboding joy as a method of minimizing vulnerability is best understood as a continuum that runs from "rehearsing tragedy" to what I call "perpetual disappointment." Some of us, like the woman in the first story, scramble to the bleakest worst-case scenario when joy rears its vulnerable head, while others never even see joy, preferring to stay in an unmoving state of perpetual disappointment. What the perpetual-disappointment folks described is this: "It's easier to live disappointed than it is to feel disappointed. It feels more vulnerable to dip in and out of disappointment than to just set up camp there. You sacrifice joy, but you suffer less pain."

Both of these ends of the continuum tell the same story: Softening into the joyful moments of our lives requires vulnerability. If, like me, you've ever stood over your children and thought to yourself, *I love you so much I can barely breathe*, and in that exact moment have been flooded with images of something terrible happening to your child, know that you're not crazy nor are you alone. About eighty percent of the parents I've interviewed acknowledged having that experience. The same percentage holds true for the thousands of parents I've spoken to and worked with over the years. Why? What are we doing and why on earth are we doing it?

Once we make the connection between vulnerability and joy, the answer is pretty straightforward: We're trying to beat vulnerability to the punch. We don't want to be blindsided by hurt. We don't want to be caught off-guard, so we literally practice being devastated or never move from self-elected disappointment.

For those of us who rehearse tragedy, there's a reason

those images flood into our mind the second we're over-whelmed with joy. When we spend our lives (knowingly or unknowingly) pushing away vulnerability, we can't hold space open for the uncertainty, risk, and emotional exposure of joy. For many of us, there's even a physiological response—a "coming out of our skin" feeling. We're desperate for more joy, but at the same time we can't tolerate the vulnerability.

And our culture assists in this doom-filled rehearsal: Most of us have a stockpile of terrible images that we can pull from at the instant we're grappling with vulnerability. I often ask audience members to raise their hands if they've seen a graphically violent image in the past week. About twenty per-cent of the audience normally raises their hands. Then I re-frame the question: "Raise your hand if you've watched the news, *CSI*, *NCIS*, *Law & Order*, *Bones*, or any other crime show on TV." At that point about eighty to ninety percent of the audience hands go up. We have the images we need to activate foreboding joy right at our neurological fingertips.

We're visual people. We trust, consume, and mentally store what we see. I remember recently being in the car with Steve and the kids as we headed to San Antonio for a long weekend. Charlie was performing his new kindergarten knock-knock joke routine for us, and we were all cracking up—even his older sister. I started welling up with joy, and in the split second that vulnerability, joy's constant companion, hit me, I shuddered, recalling an image from the news that showed an overturned SUV on I-10 and two empty car seats lying on the ground next to the truck. My laughter turned to panic, and I remember blurting out, "Slow down, Steve." He looked at me with a puzzled expression and said, "We're stopped."

DARING GREATLY: PRACTICING GRATITUDE

Even those of us who have learned to "lean into" joy and embrace our experiences are not immune to the uncomfortable quake of vulnerability that often accompanies joyful moments. We've just learned how to use it as a reminder rather than a warning shot. What was the most surprising (and life changing) difference for me was the nature of that reminder: For those welcoming the experience, the shudder of vulnerability that accompanies joy is an invitation to practice gratitude, to acknowledge how truly grateful we are for the person, the beauty, the connection, or simply the moment before us.

Gratitude, therefore, emerged from the data as the antidote to foreboding joy. In fact, every participant who spoke about the ability to stay open to joy also talked about the importance of practicing gratitude. This pattern of association was so thoroughly prevalent in the data that I made a commitment as a researcher not to talk about joy without talking about gratitude.

It wasn't just the relationship between joy and gratitude that took me by surprise. I was also startled by the fact that research participants consistently described both joyfulness and gratitude as spiritual practices that were bound to a belief in human connectedness and a power greater than us. Their stories and descriptions expanded on this, pointing to a clear distinction between happiness and joy. Participants described happiness as an emotion that's connected to circumstances, and they described joy as a spiritual way of engaging with the world that's connected to practicing gratitude. While I was initially taken aback by the relationship between joy and vulnerability, it now makes perfect sense to me, and I can see why gratitude would be the antidote to foreboding joy.

Scarcity and fear drive foreboding joy. We're afraid that the feeling of joy won't last, or that there won't be enough, or that the transition to disappointment (or whatever is in store for us next) will be too difficult. We've learned that giving in to joy is, at best, setting ourselves up for disappointment and, at worst, inviting disaster. And we struggle with the worthiness issue. Do we deserve our joy, given our inadequacies and imperfections? What about the starving children and the war-ravaged world? Who are we to be joyful?

If the opposite of scarcity is enough, then practicing gratitude is how we acknowledge that there's enough and that we're enough. I use the word practicing because the research participants spoke of tangible gratitude practices, more than merely having an attitude of gratitude or feeling grateful. In fact, they gave specific examples of gratitude practices that included everything from keeping gratitude journals and gratitude jars to implementing family gratitude rituals.

Actually, I learned the most about gratitude practices and the relationship between scarcity and joy that plays out in vulnerability from the men and women who had experienced some of the most profound losses or survived the greatest traumas. These included parents whose children had died, family members with terminally ill loved ones, and genocide and trauma survivors. One of the questions I'm most often asked is "Don't you get really depressed talking to people about vulnerability and hearing about people's darkest struggles?" My answer is *no, never.* That's because I've learned more about worthiness, resilience, and joy from those people who courageously shared their struggles with me than from any other part of my work.

And nothing has been a greater gift to me than the three

lessons I learned about joy and light from people who have spent time in sorrow and darkness:

1. **Joy comes to us in moments—ordinary moments. We risk missing out on joy when we get too busy chasing down the extraordinary.** Scarcity culture may keep us afraid of living small, ordinary lives, but when you talk to people who have survived great losses, it is clear that joy is not a constant. Without exception, all the participants who spoke to me about their losses, and what they missed the most, spoke about ordinary moments. "If I could come downstairs and see my husband sitting at the table and cursing at the newspaper . . ." "If I could hear my son giggling in the backyard . . ." "My mom sent me the craziest texts— she never knew how to work her phone. I'd give anything to get one of those texts right now."

2. **Be grateful for what you have.** When I asked people who had survived tragedy how we can cultivate and show more compassion for people who are suffering, the answer was always the same: Don't shrink away from the joy of your child because I've lost mine. Don't take what you have for granted—celebrate it. Don't apologize for what you have. Be grateful for it and share your gratitude with others. Are your parents healthy? Be thrilled. Let them know how much they mean to you. *When you honor what you have, you're honoring what I've lost.*

3. **Don't squander joy.** We can't prepare for tragedy and loss. When we turn every opportunity to feel joy into a test drive for despair, we actually diminish our resilience. Yes, softening into joy is uncomfortable. Yes, it's scary. Yes, it's vulnerable. *But every time we allow ourselves to lean into joy and give in to those moments, we build resilience and we cultivate hope.* The joy becomes part of who we are, and when bad things happen—and they do happen—we are stronger.

It took me a couple of years to understand and integrate this information, and to start to cultivate a gratitude practice. Ellen, on the other hand, seemed to intuitively understand the importance of acknowledging and owning joy. When she was in the first grade, we played hooky one afternoon and spent the day at the park. At one point we were on a paddleboat, feeding ducks stale bread that we had brought from home, when I realized that she had stopped pedaling and was sitting perfectly still in her seat. Her hands were wrapped around the bread sack, her head was tilted back, and her eyes were closed. The sun was shining on her uplifted face and she had a quiet smile on her face. I was so struck by her beauty and her vulnerability that I could barely catch my breath.

I watched for a full minute, but when she didn't move, I got a little nervous. "Ellie? Is everything okay, sweetie?"

Her smile widened and she opened her eyes. She looked at me and said, "I'm fine, Mama. I was just making a picture memory."

I had never heard of a picture memory, but I liked the sound of it. "What's that mean?"

"Oh, a picture memory is a picture I take in my mind when I'm really, really happy. I close my eyes and take a picture, so when I'm feeling sad or scared or lonely, I can look at my picture memories."

I'm not as eloquent or poised as my then six-year-old daughter, but I've been practicing. For me, expressing gratitude is still bumpier than it is graceful or fluid. I still get overwhelmed with vulnerability in the midst of joyful experiences. But now I've learned to literally say aloud, "I'm feeling vulnerable and I'm so grateful for _____."

Okay, this can be fairly awkward in the middle of a conversation, but it's much better than the alternative—catastrophizing and controlling. Just recently, Steve told me that he was thinking about taking the kids to his family's farmhouse in Pennsylvania while I was out of town for work. I immediately thought it was a great idea, until I started boarding the crazy train of *Oh, my God, I can't let them fly without me; what if something happens?* Rather than picking a fight, being critical, or making up something to quash the idea without revealing my unreasonable fears (e.g., "That's a terrible idea. Airfare is really high right now," or, "That's selfish. I want to go too."), I just said, "Vulnerability. Vulnerability. I'm grateful for . . . for . . . the kids getting to spend alone time with you and explore the country outside."

Steve smiled. He's well aware of my practice, and he knew I meant it. Before I put this research on countering foreboding joy into practice, I never knew how to get past that immediate vulnerability shudder. I didn't have the information to get from what I feared, to how I actually felt, and to what I really craved: gratitude-fueled joy.

THE SHIELD: PERFECTIONISM

One of my favorite features on my blog is my *Inspiration Interviews* series. It's special to me because I only interview people whom I find truly inspirational—people who engage with the world in a way that inspires me to be more creative and a little bit braver with my own work. I've always asked interviewees the same group of questions, and after the Wholehearted research emerged, I started asking questions about vulnerability and perfectionism. As a recovering perfectionist and an aspiring good-enough-ist, I'm always finding myself skimming down the list to read the answer to this question first: *Is perfectionism an issue for you? If so, what's one of your strategies for managing it?*

I ask this question because, in all of my data collecting, I've never heard one person attribute their joy, success, or Wholeheartedness to being perfect. In fact, what I've heard over and over throughout the years is one clear message: "The most valuable and important things in my life came to me when I cultivated the courage to be vulnerable, imperfect, and self-compassionate." Perfectionism is not the path that leads us to our gifts and to our sense of purpose; it's the hazardous detour.

I'm going to share a few of my favorite answers from the interviews with you, but first I want to tell you about the definition of *perfectionism* that bubbled up from the data. Here's what I learned:

Like vulnerability, perfectionism has accumulated around it a considerable mythology. I think it's helpful to start by looking at what perfectionism *isn't:*

- Perfectionism is not the same thing as striving for excellence. Perfectionism is not about healthy achievement and growth. Perfectionism is a defensive move. It's the belief that if we do things perfectly and look perfect, we can minimize or avoid the pain of blame, judgment, and shame. Perfectionism is a twenty-ton shield that we lug around, thinking it will protect us, when in fact it's the thing that's really preventing us from being seen.

- Perfectionism is not self-improvement. Perfectionism is, at its core, about trying to earn approval. Most perfectionists grew up being praised for achievement and performance (grades, manners, rule following, people pleasing, appearance, sports). Somewhere along the way, they adopted this dangerous and debilitating belief system: "I am what I accomplish and how well I accomplish it. Please. Perform. Perfect." Healthy striving is self- focused: How can I improve? Perfectionism is other-focused: What will they think? Perfectionism is a hustle.

- Perfectionism is not the key to success. In fact, research shows that perfectionism hampers achievement. Perfectionism is correlated with depression, anxiety, addiction, and life paralysis or missed opportunities. The fear of failing, making mistakes, not meeting people's expectations, and being criticized keeps us outside of the arena where healthy competition and striving unfolds.

- Last, perfectionism is not a way to avoid shame. Perfectionism is a form of shame. Where we struggle with perfectionism, we struggle with shame.

After using the data to bushwhack my way through the myths, I then developed the following definition of *perfectionism:*

- Perfectionism is a self-destructive and addictive belief system that fuels this primary thought: *If I look perfect and do everything perfectly, I can avoid or minimize the painful feelings of shame, judgment, and blame.*

- Perfectionism is self-destructive simply because perfection doesn't exist. It's an unattainable goal. Perfectionism is more about perception than internal motivation, and there is no way to control perception, no matter how much time and energy we spend trying.

- Perfectionism is addictive, because when we invariably do experience shame, judgment, and blame, we often believe it's because we weren't perfect enough. Rather than questioning the faulty logic of perfectionism, we become even more entrenched in our quest to look and do everything just right.

- Perfectionism actually sets us up to feel shame, judgment, and blame, which then leads to even more shame and self-blame: "It's my fault. I'm feeling this way because I'm not good enough."

DARING GREATLY: APPRECIATING THE BEAUTY OF CRACKS

Just as our experiences of foreboding joy can be located on a continuum, I found that most of us fall somewhere on a perfectionism continuum. In other words, when it comes to hiding our flaws, managing perception, and wanting to win over folks, we're all hustling a little. For some folks, perfectionism may only emerge when they're feeling particularly vulnerable. For others, perfectionism is compulsive, chronic, and debilitating—it looks and feels like an addiction.

Regardless of where we are on this continuum, if we want freedom from perfectionism, we have to make the long journey from "What will people think?" to "I am enough." That journey begins with shame resilience, self-compassion, and owning our stories. To claim the truths about who we are, where we come from, what we believe, and the very imperfect nature of our lives, we have to be willing to give ourselves a break and appreciate the beauty of our cracks or imperfections. To be kinder and gentler with ourselves and each other. To talk to ourselves the same way we'd talk to someone we care about.

Dr. Kristin Neff, a researcher and professor at the University of Texas at Austin, runs the Self-Compassion Research Lab, where she studies how we develop and practice self-compassion. According to Neff, self-compassion has three elements: self-kindness, common humanity, and mindfulness. In her new book, *Self-Compassion: Stop Beating Yourself Up and Leave Insecurity Behind*, she defines each of these elements:

- Self-kindness: Being warm and understanding toward ourselves when we suffer, fail, or feel inadequate, rather than ignoring our pain or flagellating ourselves with self-criticism.

- Common humanity: Common humanity recognizes that suffering and feelings of personal inadequacy are part of the shared human experience—something we all go through rather than something that happens to "me" alone.

- Mindfulness: Taking a balanced approach to negative emotions so that feelings are neither suppressed nor exaggerated. We cannot ignore our pain and feel compassion for it at the same time. Mindfulness requires that we not "over-identify" with thoughts and feelings, so that we are caught up and swept away by negativity.

I love how her definition of mindfulness reminds us that being mindful also means not overidentifying with or exaggerating our feelings. For me, it's so easy to get stuck in regret or shame or self-criticism when I make a mistake. But self-compassion requires an observant and accurate perspective when feeling shame or pain. Neff has a great website where you can take a self-compassion inventory and learn more about her research. The Web address is www.self-compassion.org.

In addition to practicing self-compassion (and trust me, like gratitude and everything else worthwhile, it's a practice), we must also remember that our worthiness, that core belief that we are enough, comes only when we live inside our story. We either own our stories (even the messy ones), or we stand outside of them—denying our vulnerabilities and imperfections, orphaning the parts of us that don't fit in with who/

what we think we're supposed to be, and hustling for other people's approval of our worthiness. Perfectionism is exhausting because hustling is exhausting. It's a never-ending performance.

I want to go back now to the *Inspiration Interviews* series from my blog and share some of the responses with you. In these responses I see the beauty of being real—of embracing the cracks—and I'm inspired by the self-compassion. I think they'll inspire you too. The first is from Gretchen Rubin, the best-selling writer whose book *The Happiness Project* is the account of the year she spent test-driving studies and theories about how to be happier. Her new book, *Happier at Home*, focuses on the factors that matter at home, such as possessions, marriage, time, parenthood, neighborhood. Here's how she answered the question about managing perfectionism:

> I remind myself, "Don't let the perfect be the enemy of the good." (Cribbed from Voltaire.) A twenty-minute walk that I do is better than the four-mile run that I don't do. The imperfect book that gets published is better than the perfect book that never leaves my computer. The dinner party of take-out Chinese food is better than the elegant dinner that I never host.

Andrea Scher is a photographer, writer, and life coach living in Berkeley, California. Through her e-courses "Superhero Photo" and "Mondo Beyondo" and her award-winning blog *Superhero Journal*, Andrea inspires others to live authentic, colorful, and creative lives. You can often find her sitting on the kitchen floor, holding her new baby, and asking her

four-year-old son to leap so she can take a superhero portrait.
She writes here about perfectionism (I love her mantras!):

> I was a competitive gymnast as a kid, got
> perfect attendance every year in school, was
> terrified of getting anything worse than an A
> minus, and had an eating disorder in high
> school.
>
> Oh, and I think I was the homecoming
> queen.
>
> Yep. I think I have some issues with perfec-
> tionism!
>
> But I have been working on it. As a kid, I
> equated being perfect with being loved . . .
> and I think I still confuse the two. I often find
> myself doing what Brené calls "the hustle for
> worthiness." That dance we do so that people
> don't see how incredibly flawed and human
> we are. Sometimes I have my self-worth
> wrapped up in what I do and how good I look
> doing it, but mostly I am learning to let go.
> Parenthood has taught me a lot about that. It's
> messy and humbling, and I am learning to
> show my mess.
>
> To manage my perfectionism I give myself
> tons of permission to do things that are good
> enough. I do things quickly (having two small
> children will teach you how to do most tasks
> at lightning speed), and if it's good enough, it
> gets my stamp of approval. I have a few man-
> tras that help:
>
> Quick and dirty wins the race.

Perfection is the enemy of done.
Good enough is really effin' good.

Nicholas Wilton is the artist behind the beautiful illustrations on my earlier book covers and my website. In addition to showings in gallery exhibitions and inclusion in private collections, he is the founder of the Artplane Method, a system of fundamental painting and intuition principles that help enable the creative process.

I absolutely love what he writes about perfectionism and art. It completely aligns with the research finding that perfectionism crushes creativity—which is why one of the most effective ways to start recovering from perfectionism is to start creating. Here's what Nick has to say:

> I always felt that someone, a long time ago, organized the affairs of the world into areas that made sense—categories of stuff that is perfectible, things that fit neatly in perfect bundles. The world of business, for example, is this way—line items, spreadsheets, things that add up, that can be perfected. The legal system—not always perfect, but nonetheless a mind-numbing effort to actually write down all kinds of laws and instructions that cover all aspects of being human, a kind of umbrella code of conduct we should all follow.
>
> Perfection is crucial in building an aircraft, a bridge, or a high-speed train. The code and mathematics residing just below the surface of the Internet is also this way. Things are either perfectly right or they will not work. So

much of the world we work and live in is based upon being correct, being perfect.

But after this someone got through organizing everything just perfectly, he (or probably a she) was left with a bunch of stuff that didn't fit anywhere—things in a shoe box that had to go somewhere.

So in desperation this person threw up her arms and said, "OK! Fine. All the rest of this stuff that isn't perfectible, that doesn't seem to fit anywhere else, will just have to be piled into this last, rather large, tattered box that we can sort of push behind the couch. Maybe later we can come back and figure where it all is supposed to fit in. Let's label the box ART."

The problem was thankfully never fixed, and in time the box overflowed as more and more art piled up. I think the dilemma exists because art, among all the other tidy categories, most closely resembles what it is like to be human. To be alive. It is our nature to be imperfect. To have uncategorized feelings and emotions. To make or do things that don't sometimes necessarily make sense.

Art is all just perfectly imperfect.

Once the word *Art* enters the description of what you're up to, it is almost like getting a hall pass from perfection. It thankfully releases us from any expectation of perfection.

In relation to my own work not being perfect, I just always point to the tattered box behind the couch and mention the word *Art*, and people seem to understand and let you off the hook about being perfect and go back to their business.

There's a quote that I share every time I talk about vulnerability and perfectionism. My fixation with these words from Leonard Cohen's song "Anthem" comes from how much comfort and hope they give me as I put "enough" into practice: "There's a crack in everything. That's how the light gets in."

THE SHIELD: NUMBING

If you're wondering if this section is about addiction and you're thinking, *This isn't about me*, please read on. This is about all of us. First, one of the most universal numbing strategies is what I call *crazy-busy*. I often say that when they start having twelve-step meetings for busy-aholics, they'll need to rent out football stadiums. We are a culture of people who've bought into the idea that if we stay busy enough, the truth of our lives won't catch up with us.

Second, statistics dictate that there are very few people who haven't been affected by addiction. I believe we all numb our feelings. We may not do it compulsively and chronically, which is addiction, but that doesn't mean that we don't numb our sense of vulnerability. And numbing vulnerability is especially debilitating because it doesn't just deaden the pain of our difficult experiences; numbing vulnerability also dulls our experiences of love, joy, belonging, creativity, and empathy. We can't selectively numb emotion. Numb the dark and you numb the light.

If you're also wondering if numbing refers to doing illegal drugs or having a few glasses of wine after work—the answer is yes. I'm going to argue that we need to examine the idea of "taking the edge off," and that means considering the glasses of wine we drink while we're cooking dinner, eating dinner, and cleaning up after dinner, our sixty-hour workweeks, the sugar, the fantasy football, the prescription pills, and the four shots of espresso that we drink in order to clear the fog from the wine and Advil PM. I'm talking about you and me and the stuff we do every day.

When I looked at the data, my primary question was "What are we numbing and why?" Americans today are more debt-ridden, obese, medicated, and addicted than we ever have been. For the first time in history, the Centers for Disease Control and Prevention (CDC) has announced that automobile accidents are now the second leading cause of accidental death in the United States. The leading cause? Drug overdoses. In fact, more people die from prescription drug overdoses than from heroin, cocaine, and methamphetamine drug use combined. Even more alarming is the estimate that less than 5 percent of those who died from prescription drug overdoses obtained their drugs from the folks we normally think of as street-corner drug dealers. The dealers today are more likely to be parents, relatives, friends, and physicians. Clearly there's a problem. We're desperate to feel less or more of something— to make something go away or to have more of something else.

Having spent years working closely with addiction researchers and clinicians, I had guessed that the primary driver of numbing would be our struggles with worthiness and shame: We numb the pain that comes from feeling inadequate and "less than." But that was only part of the puzzle. Anxiety and disconnection also emerged as drivers of numbing in addition to shame. As I'll explain, the most powerful need for numbing seems to come from combinations of all three—shame, anxiety, and disconnection.

The anxiety described by the research participants appeared to be fueled by uncertainty, overwhelming and competing demands on our time, and (one of the big surprises) social discomfort. Disconnection was tougher to nail down. I thought about using the term *depression* rather than *disconnection*, but as I recoded the data, that's not what I heard. I instead heard a range of experiences that encompassed depression but also included loneliness, isolation, disengagement, and emptiness.

Again, what was really powerful for me, personally and professionally, was seeing the strong pattern of shame threading through the experiences of anxiety and/or disconnection. The most accurate answers to the question about what drives numbing sound more like the answers to "What's your sign?" *Anxiety with shame rising. Disconnection with shame rising. Anxiety and disconnection with shame rising.*

Shame enters for those of us who experience anxiety because not only are we feeling fearful, out of control, and incapable of managing our increasingly demanding lives, but eventually our anxiety is compounded and made unbearable by our belief that if we were just smarter, stronger, or better, we'd be able to handle everything. Numbing here becomes a way to take the edge off of both instability and inadequacy.

With disconnection it's a similar story. We may have a couple of hundred friends on Facebook, plus a slew of colleagues, real-life friends, and neighbors, but we feel alone and unseen. Because we are hardwired for connection, disconnection always creates pain. Feeling disconnected can be a normal part of life and relationships, but when coupled with the shame of believing that we're disconnected because we're not worthy of connection, it creates a pain that we want to numb.

One stop beyond disconnection is isolation, which presents real danger. Jean Baker Miller and Irene Stiver, relational-cultural theorists from the Stone Center at Wellesley College, have eloquently captured the extremity of isolation. They write, "We believe that the most terrifying and destructive feeling that a person can experience is psychological isolation. This is not the same as being alone. It is a feeling that one is locked out of the possibility of human connection and of being powerless to change the situation. In the extreme, psychological isolation can lead to a sense of hopelessness and desperation. People will do almost anything to escape this combination of condemned isolation and powerlessness."

The part of this definition that is critical to understanding shame is the sentence "People will do almost anything to escape this combination of condemned isolation and powerlessness." Shame often leads to desperation. And reactions to this desperate need to escape from isolation and fear can run the gamut from numbing to addiction, depression, self-injury, eating disorders, bullying, violence, and suicide.

As I thought back on my own numbing history, understanding how shame magnifies anxiety and disconnection provided me with answers to questions that I've had for years. I didn't start drinking to drown my sorrows: I just needed something to do with my hands. In fact, I'm convinced that if smart phones and the bejeweled Chihuahuas that today's celebrities sport as accessories had been in fashion when I was in my late teens, I never would have started smoking and drinking. I drank and smoked to minimize my feelings of vulnerability and to look busy when all of the other girls at my table had been asked to dance. I literally needed something to do, something to help me look busy.

Twenty-five years ago it felt as if my only choice was nursing a beer, stirring an amaretto sour, or fiddling with a cigarette. I was alone at the table with no one and nothing to keep me company except for my vices. For me, vulnerability led to anxiety, which led to shame, which led to disconnection, which led to Bud Light. For many of us, the literal chemical anesthetizing of emotions is just a pleasant, albeit dangerous, side effect of behaviors that are more about fitting in, finding connection, and managing anxiety.

I quit drinking and smoking sixteen years ago. In *The Gifts of Imperfection*, I write:

> I wasn't raised with the skills and emotional practice needed to "lean into discomfort," so over time I basically became a take-the-edge-off-aholic. But they don't have meetings for that. And after some brief experimenting, I learned that describing your addiction that way in a traditional twelve-step meeting doesn't always go over very well with the purists.
>
> For me, it wasn't just the dance halls, cold beer, and Marlboro Lights of my youth that got out of hand—it was banana bread, chips and queso, e-mail, work, staying busy, incessant worrying, planning, perfectionism, and anything else that could dull those agonizing and anxiety-fueled feelings of vulnerability.

Let's look at the Daring Greatly strategies for numbing.

DARING GREATLY: SETTING BOUNDARIES, FINDING TRUE COMFORT, AND CULTIVATING SPIRIT

When I interviewed the research participants, whom I'd describe as living a Wholehearted life, about numbing, they consistently talked about three things:

1. Learning how to actually feel their feelings.
2. Staying mindful about numbing behaviors (they struggled too).
3. Learning how to lean into the discomfort of hard emotions.

This all made perfect sense to me, but I wanted to know exactly how you lean into anxiety and disconnection. So I started interviewing people about this question specifically. As I expected, there was more to it. These folks had elevated "enough" to whole new levels. Yes, they practiced mindfulness and leaning, but they also set serious boundaries in their lives.

As I asked more pointed questions about the choices and behaviors Wholehearted men and women made to reduce anxiety, they explained that reducing anxiety meant paying attention to how much they could do and how much was too much, and learning how to say, "Enough." They got very clear on what was important to them and when they could let something go.

In Sir Ken Robinson's wonderful 2010 TED talk on the learning revolution, he starts to explain to the audience that he divides the world into two groups, then he stops himself and with great humor says, "Jeremy Bentham, the great utilitarian philosopher, once spiked this argument. He said, 'There are two types of people in the world, those who divide people into two types, and those who do not.'"

Robinson paused and smiled. "Well, I do." I loved that because as a researcher, I do too. But before I talk about the two groups I identified, I want to say that this division is not exactly as neat and tidy as two discrete groups, and at the same time it almost is. Let's take a look.

When it comes to anxiety, we all struggle. Yes, there are different types of anxiety and certainly different intensities. Some anxiety is hardwired and best addressed with a combination of medication and therapy, and some of it is environmental—we're overextended and overstressed. What was interesting to me was how the participants could be divided into two camps: Group A defined the challenge of anxiety as *finding ways to manage and soothe the anxiety*, while Group B clearly defined the problem as *changing the behaviors that led to anxiety*. Participants from both groups often used today's dominating technology as an example of an anxiety-producing source during the interviews, so let's look at how these two groups thought differently about the daily onslaught of e-mail, voicemail, and text messages.

Group A: "I make a pot of coffee after I tuck in my kids so I can take care of all the e-mails between ten P.M. and midnight. If there are too many, I wake up at four A.M. and start over again. I don't like getting to work with any unanswered e-mail in my in-box. I'm exhausted, but they're answered."

Group B: "I've simply stopped sending unnecessary e-mails and asked my friends and colleagues to do the same. I've also started setting the expectation that it might take me a few days to respond. If it's important, call me. Don't text or e-mail. Call. Better yet, stop by my office."

Group A: "I use red lights, grocery lines, and elevator rides to stay on top of my calls. I even sleep with my phone in case someone calls or I remember something in the middle of the night. One time I called my assis-tant at four A.M. because I remembered that we needed to add something to a motion that we were preparing. I was surprised that she answered, but then she reminded me that I had told her to keep her phone on her night-stand. I'll rest and let off steam when we're done. Work hard. Play hard. That's my motto. And it doesn't take much to play hard when you haven't slept in a while."

Group B: "My boss, my friends, and my family know that I don't take calls before nine A.M. or after nine P.M. If the phone rings after or before those times, it's either a wrong number or an emergency—a real emergency, not a work issue."

The participants who struggled the most with numbing, Group A, explained that reducing anxiety meant finding ways to numb it, not changing the thinking, behaviors, or emotions that created anxiety. I hated every minute of this part of the research. I've always looked for better ways to manage my exhaustion and anxiety. I wanted help "living like this," not suggestions on how to "stop living like this." My struggle mirrored the struggle that I heard from the folks who talked the most about numbing. The smaller group, Group B—the participants who addressed anxiety at the root by aligning their lives with their values and setting boundaries—fell on the Wholehearted continuum.

When we asked that group about the process of setting boundaries and limits to lower the anxiety in their lives, they didn't hesitate to connect worthiness with boundaries. We have to believe we are enough in order to say, "Enough!" For women, setting boundaries is difficult because the shame gremlins are quick to weigh in: "Careful saying no. You'll really disappoint these folks. Don't let them down. Be a good girl. Make everyone happy." For men, the gremlins whisper, "Man up. A real guy could take this on and then some. Is the little mamma's boy just too tired?"

We know that *daring greatly* means engaging with our vulnerability, which can't happen when shame has the upper hand, and the same is true for dealing with anxiety-fueled disconnection. The two most powerful forms of connection are love and belonging—they are both irreducible needs of men, women, and children. As I conducted my interviews, I realized that only one thing separated the men and women who felt a deep sense of love and belonging from the people who seemed to be struggling for it. That one thing was the belief in their worthiness. It's as simple and complicated as this: If we want to fully experience love and belonging, we must believe that we are worthy of love and belonging. But before we talk more about numbing and disconnection, I want to share two more definitions with you. I shared my definition of love on page 105, here are the definitions of connection and belonging that emerged from the data.

Connection: Connection is the energy that is created between people when they feel seen, heard, and valued; when they can give and receive without judgment.

Belonging: Belonging is the innate human desire to be part of something larger than us. Because this yearning is so primal, we often try to acquire it by fitting in and by seeking approval, which are not only hollow substitutes for belonging, but often barriers to it. Because true belonging only happens when we present our authentic, imperfect selves to the world, our sense of belonging can never be greater than our level of self-acceptance.

These definitions are crucial to understanding how we become disconnected in our lives and how to change. Living a connected life ultimately is about setting boundaries, spending less time and energy hustling and winning over people who don't matter, and seeing the value of working on cultivating connection with family and close friends.

Before I undertook this research, my question was "What's the quickest way to make these feelings go away?" Today my question is "What are these feelings and where did they come from?" Invariably, the answers are that I'm not feeling connected enough to Steve or the kids, and that this comes from (take your pick) not sleeping enough, not playing enough, working too much, or trying to run from vulnerability. What has changed for me is that I know now that I can address these answers.

THE CARE AND FEEDING OF OUR SPIRITS

One final question remains, and I hear it a lot. People often ask, "Where is the line between pleasure or comfort and numbing?" In response, author and personal growth teacher Jennifer Louden has named our numbing devices "shadow comforts." When we're anxious, disconnected, vulnerable, alone, and feeling helpless, the booze and food and work and endless hours online feel like comfort, but in reality they're only casting their long shadows over our lives.

In her book *The Life Organizer*, Louden writes, "Shadow comforts can take any form. It's not what you do; it's *why* you do it that makes the difference. You can eat a piece of chocolate as a holy wafer of sweetness—a real comfort—or you can cram an entire chocolate bar into your mouth without even tasting it in a frantic attempt to soothe yourself—a shadow comfort. You can chat on message boards for half an hour and be energized by community and ready to go back to work, or you can chat on message boards because you're avoiding talking to your partner about how angry he or she made you last night."

I found that what emerged from the data was exactly what Louden points out: "It's not what you do; it's why you do it that makes the difference." The invitation is to think about the intention behind our choices and, if helpful, to discuss these issues with family, close friends, or a helping professional. There aren't any checklists or norms to help you identify shadow comforts or other destructive numbing behavior. This requires self-examination and reflection. Additionally, I would recommend listening with great care if the people you love say that they are concerned about you engaging in these types of behaviors. But ultimately these are questions that transcend what we know and how we feel—they're about our spirit. *Are my choices comforting and nourishing my spirit, or are they temporary reprieves from vulnerability and difficult emotions ultimately diminishing my spirit? Are my choices leading to my Wholeheartedness, or do they leave me feeling empty and searching?*

For me, sitting down to a wonderful meal is nourishment and pleasure. Eating while I'm standing, be it in front of the refrigerator or inside the pantry, is always a red flag. Sitting down to watch one of my favorite shows on television is pleasure. Flipping through channels for an hour is numbing.

As we think about nourishing or diminishing our spirit, we have to consider how our numbing behaviors affect the people around us—even strangers. A couple of years ago, I wrote an op-ed about cell phones and disconnection for the *Houston Chronicle* after witnessing how our crazy-busy, anxiety-fueled lifestyles affect other people. Food for thought:

Last week, while I was trying to enjoy my manicure, I watched in horror as the two women across from me talked on their phones the entire time they were getting their nails done. They employed head nods, eyebrow raises, and finger-pointing to instruct the manicurists on things like nail length and polish choices.

I really couldn't believe it.

I've had my nails done by the same two women for ten years. I know their names (their real Vietnamese names), their children's names, and many of their stories. They know my name, my children's names, and many of my stories. When I finally made a comment about the women on their cell phones, they both quickly averted their eyes. Finally, in a whisper, the manicurist said, "They don't know. Most of them don't think of us as people."

On the way home, I stopped at Barnes & Noble to pick up a magazine. The woman ahead of me in line bought two books, applied for a new "reader card," and asked to get one book gift-wrapped without getting off of her cell phone. She plowed through the entire exchange without making eye contact or directly speaking to the young woman working at the counter. She never acknowledged the presence of the human being across from her.

After leaving Barnes & Noble, I went to a drive-through fast food restaurant to get a Diet Dr Pepper. Right as I pulled up to the window, my cell phone rang. I wasn't quite sure, but I thought it might be Charlie's school calling, so I answered it. It wasn't the school—it was someone calling to confirm an appointment. I got off the phone as quickly as I could.

In the short time it took me to say, "Yes, I'll be at my appointment," the woman in the window and I had finished our soda-for-money transaction. I apologized to her the second I got off of the phone. I said, "I'm so sorry. The phone rang right when I was pulling up and I thought it was my son's school."

I must have surprised her because she got huge tears in her eyes and said, "Thank you. Thank you so much. You have no idea how humiliating it is sometimes. They don't even see us."

I don't know how it feels for her, but I do know how it feels to be an invisible member of the service industry. It can suck. I worked my way through undergrad and some of graduate school by waiting tables and bartending. I worked in a very nice restaurant that was close to campus and a hot spot for wealthy college kids and their parents (parents who were visiting for the weekend and treating their kids and their kids' friends to dinner). I was in my late twenties and praying to finish my bachelor's degree before I hit thirty.

When the customers were kind and respectful, it was OK, but one "waiter as object" moment could tear me apart. Unfortunately, I now see those moments happening all of the time.

I see adults who don't even look at their waiters when they speak to them. I see parents who let their young children talk down to store clerks. I see people rage and scream at receptionists, then treat the bosses/doctors/bankers with the utmost respect.

And I see the insidious nature of race, class, and privilege playing out in one of the most historically damaging ways possible—the server/served relationship.

Everyone wants to know why customer service has gone to hell in a handbasket. I want to know why customer behavior has gone to hell in a handbasket.

When we treat people as objects, we dehumanize them. We do something really terrible to their souls and to our own. Martin Buber, an Austrian-born philosopher, wrote about the differences between an I-it relationship and an I-you relationship. An I-it relationship is basically what we create when we are in transactions with people whom we treat like objects—people who are simply there to serve us or complete a task. I-you relationships are characterized by human connection and empathy.

Buber wrote, "When two people relate to each other authentically and humanly, God is the electricity that surges between them."

After spending a decade studying belonging, authenticity, and shame, I can say for certain that we are hardwired for connection—emotionally, physically, and spiritually. I'm not suggesting that we engage in a deep, meaningful relationship with the man who works at the cleaners or the woman who works at the drive-through, but I am suggesting that we stop dehumanizing people and start looking them in the eye when we speak to them. If we don't have the energy or time to do that, we should stay at home.

Spirituality emerged as a fundamental guidepost in Wholeheartedness. Not religiosity but the deeply held belief that we are inextricably connected to one another by a force greater than ourselves—a force grounded in love and compassion. For some of us that's God, for others it's nature, art, or even human soulfulness. I believe that owning our worthiness is the act of acknowledging that we are sacred. Perhaps embracing vulnerability and overcoming numbing is ultimately about the care and feeding of our spirits.

THE LESS FREQUENTED SHELVES IN THE ARMORY

So far, we've cracked open the armory doors to throw some light on the common arsenal that pretty much everyone uses to keep themselves safe from vulnerability. Foreboding joy, perfectionism, and numbing have emerged as the three most universal methods of protection—what we call major categories of defense. In this last part of the chapter, I want to briefly explore the less frequented shelves in the armory where a few more masks and pieces that form important subcategories of shielding are kept. Most of us are likely to identify with one or more of these protection mechanisms, or, at the very least, we will see slivers of ourselves reflected back from their polished surfaces in a way that cultivates some understanding.

THE SHIELD: VIKING OR VICTIM

I recognized this piece of armor when a significant group of research participants indicated they had very little use for the concept of vulnerability. Their responses to the idea that vulnerability might have value ranged from dismissive and defensive to hostile. What emerged from these interviews and interactions was a lens on the world that essentially saw people divided into two groups (ahem, like me and Sir Ken Robinson) that I call *Vikings* or *Victims*.

Unlike some participants who had intellectual or theoretical issues with the value of vulnerability, these folks shared the belief that everyone without exception belongs to one of two mutually exclusive groups: Either you're a Victim in life—a sucker or a loser who's always being taken advantage of and can't hold your own—or you're a Viking—someone who sees the threat of being victimized as a constant, so you stay in control, you dominate, you exert power over things, and you never show vulnerability.

As I coded the data from these interviews, I kept thinking about the chapter in my dissertation on the French philosopher Jacques Derrida and binary opposition (the pairing of related terms that are opposite). While the respondents didn't all use the same examples, a strong pattern of paired opposites emerged in the language they used to describe their worldview: winner or loser, survive or die, kill or be killed, strong or weak, leaders or followers, success or failure, crush or be crushed. And in case those aren't clear enough examples, there's the life motto of a high-achieving, take-no-prisoners lawyer, "The world is divided into assholes and suckers. It's that simple."

The source of their Viking-or-Victim worldview was not completely clear, but most attributed it to the values they had been taught growing up, the experience of surviving hardships, or their professional training. The majority of the participants who fell into the group holding this view were men, but there were also women. It makes sense that this is a somewhat gendered issue as many men, even men who don't rely on this armor, talked about the win-lose-zero-sum-power dynamic being taught and modeled as they grew up. And, don't forget, winning, dominance, and power over women were part of the list of masculine norms that we discussed in Chapter 3.

In addition to socialization and life experiences, many of these folks held jobs or worked in cultures that reinforced the Viking-or-Victim mentality: We heard this from servicemen and -women, veterans, corrections and law-enforcement officers, and people working in high-performance, supercompetitive cultures like law, technology, and finance. What I don't know is if these folks sought careers that leveraged their existing Viking-or-Victim belief system, or if their work experiences shaped this win-or-lose take on life. My guess would be that a larger percentage of folks belong to the former group, but I don't have the data to do more than speculate. It's something we're researching now.

One issue that made these interviews some of the most difficult was the honesty with which people spoke about the struggles in their personal lives—dealing with high-risk behaviors, divorces, disconnection, loneliness, addiction, anger, exhaustion. But rather than seeing these behaviors and negative outcomes as consequences of their Viking-or-Victim worldview, they perceived them as evidence of the harsh win-or-lose nature of life.

When I look at the statistics in more vulnerability-intolerant Viking-or-Victim professions, I see a dangerous pattern developing. And no place is this more evident than in the military. The statistics on post-traumatic-stress-related suicides, violence, addiction, and risk-taking all point to this haunting truth: *For soldiers serving in Afghanistan and Iraq, coming home is more lethal than being in combat.* From the invasion of Afghanistan to the summer of 2009, the US military lost 761 soldiers in combat in that country. Compare that to the 817 who took their own lives over the same period. And this number doesn't account for deaths related to violence, high-risk behaviors, and addiction.

Craig Bryan, a University of Texas psychologist and suicide expert who recently left the air force, told *Time* magazine that the military finds itself in a catch-22: "We train our warriors to use controlled violence and aggression, to suppress strong emotional reactions in the face of adversity, to tolerate physical and emotional pain, and to overcome the fear of injury and death. These qualities are also associated with increased risk for suicide." Bryan then explained that the military can't decrease the intensity of that conditioning "without negatively affecting the fighting capability of our military." And he gave chilling expression to the inherent danger of looking at the world through the Viking-or-Victim lens for those in the military when he noted, "Service members are, simply put, more capable of killing themselves by sheer consequence of their professional training." The situation may be at its most extreme in the military, but if you look at the mental and physical health statistics of police officers, you'll find the same thing.

The same holds true in organizations—when we lead, teach, or preach from a gospel of Viking or Victim, win or lose, we crush faith, innovation, creativity, and adaptability to change. Take away the guns, in fact, and we find outcomes similar to those for soldiers and police in corporate America. Lawyers—an example of a profession largely trained in win or lose, succeed or fail—have outcomes that aren't much better. The American Bar Association reports that suicides among lawyers are close to four times greater than the rate of the general population. An *American Bar Association Journal* article reported that experts on lawyer depression and substance abuse attributed the higher suicide rate to lawyers' perfectionism and on their need to be aggressive and emotionally detached. And this mentality can trickle down into our home lives as well. When we teach or model to our children that vulnerability is dangerous and should be pushed away, we lead them directly into danger and disconnection.

The Viking or Victim armor doesn't just perpetuate behaviors such as dominance, control, and power over folks who see themselves as Vikings, it can also perpetuate a sense of ongoing victimhood for people who constantly struggle with the idea that they're being targeted or unfairly treated. With this lens, there are only two possible positions that people can occupy—power over or powerless. In the interviews I heard many participants sound resigned to Victim simply because they didn't want to become the only alternative in their opinion—Vikings. Reducing our life options to such limited and extreme roles leaves very little hope for transformation and meaningful change. I think that's why there's often a sense of desperation and feeling "boxed in" around this perspective.

DARING GREATLY: REDEFINING SUCCESS, REINTEGRATING VULNERABILITY, AND SEEKING SUPPORT

To examine how the research participants moved from Viking or Victim to engaging in vulnerability, there was a clear distinction between those who operated from this belief system because it's what they learned or it's a value they hold, and those who rely on this life lens as a result of trauma. Ultimately the question that best challenges the logic behind Viking or Victim for both groups is this: How are you defining success?

It turns out that in this win-or-lose, succeed-or-fail paradigm, Vikings are not victorious by any metric that most of us would label "success." Survival or winning may be success in the midst of competition, combat, or trauma, but when the immediacy of that threat is removed, merely surviving is not living. As I mentioned earlier, love and belonging are irreducible needs of men, women, and children, and love and belonging are impossible to experience without vulnerability. Living without connection—without knowing love and belonging—is not victory. Fear and scarcity fuel the Viking-or-Victim approach and part of reintegrating vulnerability means examining shame triggers; what's fueling the win-or-lose fear? The men and women who made the shift from this paradigm to Wholeheartedness all talked about cultivating trust and connection in relationships as a prerequisite for trying on a less-combative way of engaging with the world.

As far as connection and the military is concerned, I'm not advocating for a kinder, gentler fighting force—I understand the realities faced by nations and the soldiers who protect them. What I *am* advocating is a kinder, gentler public, one willing to embrace, support, and reach out to the men and women we pay to be invulnerable on our behalf. *Are we willing to reach out and connect?*

A great example of how connection can heal and transform is the work being done by Team Red, White and Blue (TeamRWB.org). According to their mission statement, they believe the most effective way to impact a veteran's life is through a meaningful relationship with someone in their community. Their program pairs wounded veterans with local volunteers. Together, they share meals, attend the veteran's medical appointments, go to local sporting events, and engage in other social activities. This interaction allows veterans to grow in their community, meet supportive people, and find new passions in life.

My interest in this work not only stemmed from my research, but also from an extraordinary experience I had working with a group of veterans and military family members on a shame resilience project in one of my classes at the University of Houston. It changed my life. It made me realize how much we, the public, can do for veterans, and why our politics and beliefs about war shouldn't stop us from reaching out to them with vulnerability, compassion, and connection. I will always be grateful for that experience and for what I've learned interviewing veterans about their experiences. For many of us who grieve over the wounds of war, we're missing an opportunity for healing that's right in front of us. Team RWB's motto, *It's Our Turn!*, is a call to action for all of us who want to do something to support vets. I'm working with them now and I invite everyone to find a way to reach out. *Dare greatly and take actions that communicate to veterans or military families that they are not alone. Actions that communicate, "Your struggle is my struggle. Your trauma is my trauma. Your healing is my healing."*

TRAUMA AND DARING GREATLY

We all struggle to understand why some people who have survived trauma—be it combat, domestic violence, sexual or physical abuse, or the quieter but equally devastating covert traumas of oppression, neglect, isolation, or living in extreme fear or stress—exhibit tremendous resilience and lead full, Wholehearted lives, while others become defined by their trauma. They may become perpetrators themselves of the violence they suffered, they struggle with addiction, or they're unable to escape the feeling that they are victims in situations where they're not.

After studying shame for six years, I knew that part of the answer was shame resilience—the people with the most resilience intentionally cultivated the four elements that we discussed in the earlier chapters. The other part of the answer felt elusive to me until I started my new research interviewing people about Wholeheartedness and vulnerability. Then it made perfect sense. If we're forced into seeing the world through the Viking-or-Victim lens as a survival mechanism, then it can feel impossible or even deadly to let go of that worldview. How can we expect someone to give up a way of seeing and understanding the world that has physically, cognitively, or emotionally kept them alive? None of us is ever able to part with our survival strategies without significant support and the cultivation of replacement strategies. Putting down the Viking-or-Victim shield often requires help from a professional—someone who understands trauma. Groups are also very helpful.

The research participants who survived trauma and are living Wholehearted lives spoke passionately about the need to:

- Acknowledge the problem;

- Seek professional help and/or support;

- Work through the accompanying shame and secrecy;

- And approach the reintegration of vulnerability as a daily practice rather than a checklist item.

And while the importance of spirituality saturated all of the interviews with the Wholehearted, it emerged as especially important with the participants who consider themselves not only trauma survivors, but also "thrivers."

THE SHIELD: LETTING IT ALL HANG OUT

I see two forms of oversharing in our culture. The first is what I call *floodlighting*, and the other is *the smash and grab*.

As we discussed in the chapter on vulnerability myths, oversharing is not vulnerability. In fact, it often results in disconnection, distrust, and disengagement.

THE SHIELD: FLOODLIGHTING

To understand floodlighting, we have to see that the intentions behind this kind of sharing are multifaceted and often include some combination of soothing one's pain, testing the loyalty and tolerance in a relationship, and/or hot-wiring a new connection ("We've only known each other for a couple of weeks, but I'm going to share this and we'll be BFFs now"). Unfortunately for all of us who've done this (and I include myself in this group), the response is normally the opposite of what we're looking for: People recoil and shut down, compounding our shame and disconnection. You can't use vulnerability to discharge your own discomfort, or as a tolerance barometer in a relationship ("I'll share this and see if you stick around"), or to fast-forward a relationship—it just won't cooperate.

Ordinarily, when we reach out and share ourselves—our fears, hopes, struggles, and joy—we create small sparks of connection. Our shared vulnerability creates light in normally dark places. My metaphor for this is twinkle lights (I keep them in my house year-round as a reminder).

There's something magical about the idea of twinkle lights shining in dark and difficult places. The lights are small, and a single light is not very special, but an entire strand of sparkling lights is sheer beauty. It's the connectivity that makes them beautiful. When it comes to vulnerability, connectivity means sharing our stories with people who have *earned the right to hear them*—people with whom we've cultivated relationships that can bear the weight of our story. Is there trust? Is there mutual empathy? Is there reciprocal sharing? Can we ask for what we need? These are the crucial connection questions.

When we share vulnerability, especially shame stories, with someone with whom there is no connectivity, their emotional (and sometimes physical) response is often to wince, as if we have shone a floodlight in their eyes. Instead of a strand of delicate lights, our shared vulnerability is blinding, harsh, and unbearable. If we are on the receiving end, our hands fly up and cover our faces, we squeeze our entire faces (not just our eyes) shut, and we look away. When it's over, we feel depleted, confused, and sometimes even manipulated. Not exactly the empathic response that those telling the story were hoping for. Even for those of us who study empathy and teach empathy skills, it's rare that we're able to stay attuned when someone's oversharing has stretched us past our connectivity with them.

DARING GREATLY: CLARIFYING INTENTIONS, SETTING BOUNDARIES, AND CULTIVATING CONNECTION

Much of the beauty of light owes its existence to the dark. The most powerful moments of our lives happen when we string together the small flickers of light created by courage, compassion, and connection and see them shine in the darkness of our struggles. That darkness is lost when we use vulnerability to floodlight our listener, and the response is disconnection. We then use this disconnection as verification that we'll never find comfort, that we're not worthy, that the relationship is no good, or, in the case of oversharing to hot-wire a connection, that we'll never have the intimacy that we crave. We think, *Vulnerability is a crock. It's not worth it and I'm not worth it.* What we don't see is that *using* vulnerability is not the same thing as *being* vulnerable; it's the opposite—it's armor.

Sometimes we're not even aware that we're oversharing as armor. We can purge our vulnerability or our shame stories out of total desperation to be heard. We blurt out something that is causing us immense pain because we can't bear the thought of holding it in for one more second. Our intentions may not be purging or blurting to armor ourselves or push others away, but that's the exact outcome of our behaviors. Whether we're on the purging end or the receiving end of this experience, self-compassion is critical. We have to give ourselves a break when we share too much too soon, and we have to practice self-kindness when we feel like we weren't able to hold space for someone who hit us with the floodlight. Judgment exacerbates disconnection.

Hearing this, sometimes people ask me how I decide what to share and how to share it when it comes to my own work. I share a lot of myself in my work, after all, and I certainly haven't cultivated trusting relationships with all of you or all of the people in the audiences where I speak. It's an important question, and the answer is that I don't tell stories or share vulnerabilities with the public until I've worked through them with the people I love. I have my own boundaries around what I share and what I don't share and I stay mindful of my intentions.

First, I only share stories or experiences that I've worked through and feel that I can share from solid ground. I don't share what I define as "intimate" stories, nor do I share stories that are fresh wounds. I did that once or twice early in my career and it was pretty terrible. There's nothing like staring into an audience of a thousand people who are all giving you the floodlight look.

Second, I follow the rule that I learned in my graduate social work training. Sharing yourself to teach or move a process forward can be healthy and effective, but disclosing information as a way to work through your personal stuff is inappropriate and unethical. Last, I only share when I have no unmet needs that I'm trying to fill. I firmly believe that being vulnerable with a larger audience is only a good idea if the healing is tied to the sharing, not to the expectations I might have for the response I get.

When I asked other people who share their stories through blogs, books, and public speaking about this, it turns out that they are very similar in their approaches and intentions. I don't want the fear of floodlighting to stop anyone from sharing their struggles with the world, but being mindful about what, why, and how we share is important when the context is a larger public. We're all grateful for people who write and speak in ways that help us remember that we're not alone.

If you recognize yourself in this shield, this checklist might help:

Why am I sharing this?

What outcome am I hoping for?

What emotions am I experiencing?

Do my intentions align with my values?

Is there an outcome, response, or lack of a response that will hurt my feelings?

Is this sharing in the service of connection?

Am I genuinely asking the people in my life for what I need?

THE SHIELD: THE SMASH AND GRAB

If floodlighting is about mis*using* vulnerability, the second form of oversharing is all about using vulnerability as a manipulation tool. A smash-and-grab job is where a burglar smashes in a door or a store window and grabs what s/he can; it's sloppy, unplanned, and desperate. The smash and grab used as vulnerability armor is about smashing through people's social boundaries with intimate information, then grabbing whatever attention and energy you can get your hands on. We see this most often in celebrity culture, where sensationalism thrives.

Unfortunately, teachers and school administrators have told me that they see this same smash-and-grab behavior in students as young as middle school kids. Unlike floodlighting, which at least comes from a place of needing confirmation of our worthiness, this purported disclosure of vulnerability feels less real. I haven't interviewed enough people who engage in this behavior to fully understand the motivation, but what's emerged so far is attention seeking. Of course, worthiness issues can and do underpin attention seeking, but in our social media world, it's increasingly difficult to determine what's a real attempt to connect and what's performance. The only thing I do know is that it's *not* vulnerability.

DARING GREATLY: QUESTIONING INTENTIONS

This self-exposure instead feels one-directional, and for those who engage in it an audience appears to be more desirable than intimate connection. If we find ourselves engaging in a smash and grab, I think the reality-check questions are the same as the ones in the section on floodlighting. I think it's also important to ask, "What need is driving this behavior?" and "Am I trying to reach, hurt, or connect with someone specifically, and is this the right way to do it?"

THE SHIELD: SERPENTINING

I'm not someone who typically enjoys slapstick humor or screwball comedies. I much prefer a good romantic comedy or one of those painfully slow, character-driven Miramax movies. That makes the movie clip that I'm using as the metaphor for this particular vulnerability protection mechanism seem odd. But honestly, every time I watch this movie, I laugh so hard that my face hurts. Just thinking about it makes me start laughing.

The movie is the 1979 comedy *The In-Laws*, starring Peter Falk and Alan Arkin. On the eve of their children's wedding, dentist Sheldon Kornpett (played by Alan Arkin) meets Vince Ricardo (played by Peter Falk). Sheldon is the bride's father, and Vince is the groom's. Arkin's character is an anxious, regimented, straitlaced dentist. Falk's character is a CIA operative who appears to have gone rogue and who thinks nothing of car chases and shootouts. As you've probably guessed, the lovable but reckless agent drags the unsuspecting dentist into his far-flung misadventures.

The movie is really corny, but Peter Falk is brilliant as the outrageous agent and Alan Arkin is the perfect uptight straight man. My very favorite scene is when Falk tells a terrified Arkin to avoid a flurry of bullets by running in a zigzag pattern. They're totally exposed on an airport runway while being shot at by multiple snipers, and his best advice is "Serpentine, Shel! Serpentine!" At one point, the dentist miraculously makes it to shelter, but then remembers that he didn't serpentine, so he runs back into the line of fire so he can zigzag his way back to cover. I'm totally into this, so I put the two-minute clip on my website. Scroll down to the bottom of the page and you'll see it (http://www.brenebrown.com/videos).

I don't know why it cracks me up, but I laugh out loud every time I see it. Maybe it's the visual of a wild-eyed Peter Falk running back and forth, yelling, "Serpentine!" Maybe it's because I remember watching it with my dad and brother and falling out. To this day if things are getting tense in a family conversation, one of us will nonchalantly say, "Serpentine," and we'll all laugh.

Serpentining is the perfect metaphor for how we spend enormous energy trying to dodge vulnerability when it would take far less effort to face it straight on. The image also conveys how fruitless it is to think of zigzagging in the face of something as expansive and all-consuming as vulnerability.

"Serpentining" means trying to control a situation, backing out of it, pretending it's not happening, or maybe even pretending that you don't care. We use it to dodge conflict, discomfort, possible confrontation, the potential for shame or hurt, and/or criticism (self- or other-inflicted). Serpentining can lead to hiding out, pretending, avoidance, procrastination, rationalizing, blaming, and lying.

I have a tendency to want to serpentine when I feel vulnerable. If I have to make a difficult call, I'll try to script both sides of it, I'll convince myself that I should wait, I'll draft an e-mail while telling myself that it's better in writing, and I'll think of a million other things to do. I'll emotionally run back and forth until I'm exhausted.

DARING GREATLY: BEING PRESENT, PAYING ATTENTION, MOVING FORWARD

When I catch myself trying to zigzag my way out of vulnerability, it always helps to have Peter Falk's voice in my head shouting, "Serpentine, Shel!" It makes me laugh, which forces me to breathe. Breathing and humor are great ways to reality-check our behaviors and to start engaging with vulnerability.

Serpentining is draining, and running back and forth to avoid something is not a good way to live. As I was trying to come up with occasions when serpentining might be useful, I thought about the advice that I once received from an old guy who lived in a Louisiana swamp. My parents took my brother and me to fish in the channels running through some swampland owned by the company my dad worked for in New Orleans. The man who let us onto the property said, "If a gator comes atcha, run a zigzag pattern—they're quick but they ain't good at making turns."

Well, a gator did lunge out of the water and ate the end off my mom's fishing pole, but we never were chased. And, as it turns out, the whole thing is a myth anyway. According to the experts at the San Diego Zoo, we can easily outrun an alligator, zigzagging or not. They max out at a speed of around ten or eleven miles per hour, and more importantly, they can't run very far. They depend on surprise attacks, not chasing down their prey. In that sense they're very much like the gremlins that live in the shame swamplands and keep us from being vulnerable. So, we don't need to serpentine; we just need to be present, pay attention, and move forward.

THE SHIELD: CYNICISM, CRITICISM, COOL, AND CRUELTY

If you decide to walk into the arena and *dare greatly*, you're going to get kicked around. It doesn't matter if your arena is politics or the PTO, or if your great dare is an article for your school newsletter, a promotion, or selling a piece of pottery on Etsy—you're going to be on the receiving end of some cynicism and criticism before it's over. There may even be some plain ol' mean-spiritedness. Why? Because cynicism, criticism, cruelty, and cool are even better than armor—they can be fashioned into weapons that not only keep vulnerability at a distance but also can inflict injury on the people who are being vulnerable and making us uncomfortable.

If we are the kind of people who "don't do vulnerability," there's nothing that makes us feel more threatened and more incited to attack and shame people than to see someone daring greatly. Someone else's daring provides an uncomfortable mirror that reflects back our own fears about showing up, creating, and letting ourselves be seen. That's why we come out swinging. When we see cruelty, vulnerability is likely to be the driver.

When I say criticism, I don't mean productive feedback, debate, and disagreement over the value or importance of a contribution. I'm talking about put-downs, personal attacks, and unsubstantiated claims about our motivations and intentions.

When I talk about cynicism, I don't mean healthy skepticism and questioning. I'm talking about the reflexive cynicism that leads to mindless responses like "That's so stupid," or "What a loser idea." Cool is one of the most rampant forms of cynicism. *Whatever. Totally Lame. So uncool. Who gives a shit?* Among some folks it's almost as if enthusiasm and engagement have become a sign of gullibility. Being too excited or invested makes you *lame*. A word that we've banned in our house along with *loser* and *stupid*.

In the introduction to the chapter I talked about adolescence as the starting line for the race to the armory. Cynicism and cool are currency of the realm in middle and high school. Every single student in my daughter's middle school wears a hoodie every single day (even when it's 95 degrees outside). Not only do these jackets shield vulnerability by being the ultimate in cool accessories, but I'm pretty sure the kids think of them as invisibility cloaks. They literally disappear inside them. They're a way to hide. When the hoods are up and the hands are hidden in the pocket, they scream disengagement. *Too cool to care.*

As adults, we can also protect ourselves from vulnerability with cool. We worry about being perceived as laughing too loud, buying in, caring too much, being too eager. We don't wear hoodies as often, but we can use our titles, education, background, and positions as handles on the shields of criticism, cynicism, cool, and cruelty: *I can talk to you this way or blow you off because of who I am or what I do for a living*. And, make no mistake, when it comes to this shield, handles are also fashioned out of nonconformity and rejection of traditional status markers: *I dismiss you because you've sold out and you spend your life in a cubicle* or *I'm more relevant and interesting because I rejected the trappings of higher education, traditional employment, etc.*

DARING GREATLY: TIGHTROPE WALKING, PRACTICING SHAME RESILIENCE, AND REALITY CHECKING

Over the course of one year, I interviewed artists, writers, innovators, business leaders, clergy, and community leaders about these issues, and how they stayed open to the constructive (albeit difficult-to-hear) criticism while filtering out the mean-spirited attacks. Basically I wanted to know how they maintained the courage to keep on walking into the arena. I'll confess that I was motivated by my own struggle to learn how to keep daring.

When we stop caring about what people think, we lose our capacity for connection. When we become defined by what people think, we lose our willingness to be vulnerable. If we dismiss all the criticism, we lose out on important feedback, but if we subject ourselves to the hatefulness, our spirits get crushed. It's a tightrope, shame resilience is the balance bar, and the safety net below is the one or two people in our lives who can help us reality-check the criticism and cynicism.

I'm very visual, so I have a picture of a person on a tightrope hanging over my desk to remind me that working to stay open and at the same time to keep boundaries in place is worth the energy and risk. I actually used a Sharpie to write this across the balance bar: "Worthiness is my birthright." It's both a reminder to practice shame resilience and a touchstone of my spiritual beliefs. And in case I'm feeling more ornery than usual, I have a little Post-it Note under my tightrope picture that reads, "Cruelty is cheap, easy, and chickenshit." That's also a touchstone of my spiritual beliefs.

The research participants who had used criticism and cynicism in the past as a way to protect themselves from vulnerability had some very powerful wisdom to share about their transition to Wholeheartedness. Many of them said that they grew up with parents who modeled that behavior and that they weren't aware of how fully they had mimicked it until they started investigating their own fear of being vulnerable, trying new things, and engaging. These folks were not egomaniacs who took pleasure in cutting down other people; in fact, they were consistently harder on themselves than they were on other people. So their mean-spiritedness wasn't only directed outward, even if they admitted that they often used it to lessen their own self-doubt.

The first sentence of the "daring greatly" quote from Theodore Roosevelt says a lot: "It's not the critic who counts." And for the men and women I interviewed who defined themselves as that critic, the "not counting" was definitely felt. They often struggled with feeling dismissed and invisible in their own lives. Criticizing was a way to be heard. When I asked how they moved from hurtful criticism to constructive criticism and from cynicism to contribution, they described a process that mirrored shame resilience: understanding what triggered their attack, what it means about their own sense of self-worth, talking to people they trust about it, and asking for what they need. Many of these folks had to dig deep about the cool issue. How did being perceived as cool become a driving value and what was the cost of pretending that things didn't matter?

The fear of being vulnerable can unleash cruelty, criticism, and cynicism in all of us. Making sure we take responsibility for what we say is one way that we can check our intentions. Dare greatly and put your name on your posted comments online. If you don't feel comfortable owning it, then don't say it. And if you're reading this and you have control over online sites that allow comments, then you should dare greatly and make users sign in and use real names, and hold the community responsible for creating a respectful environment.

In addition to walking the tightrope, practicing shame resilience, and cultivating a safety-net community that supports me when I'm feeling attacked or hurt, I've implemented two additional strategies. The first is simple: I only accept and pay attention to feedback from people who are also in the arena. If you're occasionally getting your butt kicked as you respond, and if you're also figuring out how to stay open to feedback without getting pummeled by insults, I'm more likely to pay attention to your thoughts about my work. If, on the other hand, you're not helping, contributing, or wrestling with your own gremlins, I'm not at all interested in your commentary.

The second strategy is also simple. I carry a small sheet of paper in my wallet that has written on it the names of people whose opinions of me matter. To be on that list, you have to love me for my strengths and struggles. You have to know that I'm trying to be Wholehearted, but I still cuss too much, flip people off under the steering wheel, and have both Lawrence Welk and Metallica on my iPod. You have to know and respect that I'm totally uncool. There's a great quote from the movie *Almost Famous* that says, "The only true currency in this bankrupt world is what you share with someone else when you're uncool."

To be on my list, you have to be what I call a "stretch-mark friend"—our connection has been stretched and pulled so much that it's become part of who we are, a second skin, and there are a few scars to prove it. We're totally uncool with each other. I don't think anyone has more than one or two people who qualify for that list. The important thing is not to discount the stretch-mark friends to gain the approval of the strangers who are being mean and nasty or are too cool. Nothing serves as a better reminder of that than the immortal words of my friend Scott Stratten, author of *UnMarketing*: "Don't try to win over the haters; you're not the jackass whisperer."

CHAPTER 5
MIND THE GAP:
CULTIVATING CHANGE AND CLOSING THE DISENGAGEMENT DIVIDE

Minding the gap is a daring strategy. We have to pay attention to the space between where we're actually standing and where we want to be. More importantly, we have to practice the values that we're holding out as important in our culture. Minding the gap requires both an embrace of our own vulnerability and cultivation of shame resilience—we're going to be called upon to show up as leaders and parents and educators in new and uncomfortable ways. We don't have to be perfect, just engaged and committed to aligning values with action.

MIND the Gap" first appeared in 1969 on the London Underground as a warning to train passengers to be careful while stepping over the gap between the train door and the station platform. It has since become the name of a band and a movie, and the phrase has been captured on everything from T-shirts to doormats. In our house we have a small, framed "Mind the Gap" postcard that reminds us to pay attention to the space between where we're standing and where we want to go. Let me explain.

STRATEGY VERSUS CULTURE

In the business world, there's an ongoing debate about the relationship between strategy and culture, and the relative importance of each. Just to define the terms, I think of *strategy* as "the game plan," or the detailed answer to the question "What do we want to achieve and how are we going to get there?" We all—families, religious groups, project teams, teachers from the kindergarten cluster—have game plans. And we all think about the goals we want to accomplish and the steps we need to take to be successful.

Culture, on the other hand, is less about what we want to achieve and more about who we are. Out of the many complex definitions of culture, including those that weighed down my undergrad sociology textbooks, the one that resonates the most with me is the simplest. As organizational development pioneers Terrence Deal and Allan Kennedy explained it: "Culture is the way we do things around here." I like this definition because it rings true for discussions about all cultures—from the larger culture of scarcity that I write about in the first chapter, to a specific organizational culture, to the culture that defines my family.

Some form of the debate about what's more important, strategy or culture, bubbles up in every conversation I have with leaders. One camp subscribes to the famous quote often attributed to thought leader Peter Drucker: "Culture eats strategy for breakfast." Other folks believe that pitting one against the other creates a false dichotomy and that we need both. Interestingly, I've yet to find a strong argument that strategy is more important than culture. I think everyone agrees *in theory* that "who we are" is at least as important as "what we want to achieve."

While some complain that the debate is old, and too chicken-or-the-egg to be helpful, I think it's a critically relevant discussion for organizations. Maybe more importantly, I think examining these issues can transform families, schools, and communities.

"The way we do things around here," or culture, is complex. In my experience, I can tell a lot about the culture and values of a group, family, or organization by asking these ten questions:

1. What behaviors are rewarded? Punished?
2. Where and how are people actually spending their resources (time, money, attention)?

3. What rules and expectations are followed, enforced, and ignored?

4. Do people feel safe and supported talking about how they feel and asking for what they need?

5. What are the sacred cows? Who is most likely to tip them? Who stands the cows back up?

6. What stories are legend and what values do they convey?

7. What happens when someone fails, disappoints, or makes a mistake?

8. How is vulnerability (uncertainty, risk, and emotional exposure) perceived?

9. How prevalent are shame and blame and how are they showing up?

10. What's the collective tolerance for discomfort? Is the discomfort of learning, trying new things, and giving and receiving feedback normalized, or is there a high premium put on comfort (and how does that look)?

In each of the following sections I'll talk about how these play out in our lives and what specifically I look for, but first I want to talk about where this line of questioning leads us.

As someone who studies culture as a whole, I think the power of these questions is their ability to shed light on the darkest areas of our lives: disconnection, disengagement, and our struggle for worthiness. Not only do these questions help us understand the culture, they surface the discrepancies between "what we say" and "what we do," or between the values we espouse and the values we practice. My dear friend Charles Kiley uses the term "aspirational values" to describe the elusive list of values that reside in our best intentions, on the wall of our cubical, at the heart of our parenting lectures, or in our company's vision statement. If we want to isolate the problems and develop transformation strategies, we have to hold our aspirational values up against what I call our practiced values—how we actually live, feel, behave, and think. Are we walking our talk? Answering this can get very uncomfortable.

THE DISENGAGEMENT DIVIDE

Here's my theory: Disengagement is the issue underlying the majority of problems I see in families, schools, communities, and organizations and it takes many forms, including the ones we discussed in the "Armory" chapter. We disengage to protect ourselves from vulnerability, shame, and feeling lost and without purpose. We also disengage when we feel like the people who are leading us—our boss, our teachers, our principal, our clergy, our parents, our politicians—aren't living up to their end of the social contract.

Politics is a great, albeit painful, example of *social contract disengagement*. Politicians on both sides of the aisle are making laws that they're not required to follow or that don't affect them, they're engaging in behaviors that would result in most of us getting fired, divorced, or arrested. They're espousing values that are rarely displayed in their behavior. And just watching them shame and blame each other is degrading for us. They're not living up to their side of the social contract and voter turnout statistics show that we're disengaging.

Religion is another example of social contract disengagement. First, disengagement is often the result of leaders not living by the same values they're preaching. Second, in an uncertain world, we often feel desperate for absolutes. It's the human response to fear. When religious leaders leverage our fear and need for more certainty by extracting vulnerability from spirituality and turning faith into "compliance and consequences," rather than teaching and modeling how to wrestle with the unknown and how to embrace mystery, the entire concept of faith is bankrupt on its own terms. Faith minus vulnerability equals politics, or worse, extremism. Spiritual connection and engagement is not built on compliance, it's the product of love, belonging, and vulnerability.

So, here's the question: *We don't intentionally create cultures in our families, schools, communities, and organizations that fuel disengagement and disconnection, so how does it happen? Where's the gap?*

The gap starts here: **We can't give people what we don't have. Who we are matters immeasurably more than what we know or who we want to be.**

The space between our practiced values (what we're actually doing, thinking, and feeling) and our aspirational values (what we want to do, think, and feel) is the value gap, or what I call "the disengagement divide." It's where we lose our employees, our clients, our students, our teachers, our congregations, and even our own children. We can take big steps—we can even make a running jump to cross the widening value fissures that we face at home, work, and school—but at some point, when that divide broadens to a certain critical degree, we're goners. That's why dehumanizing cultures foster the highest levels of disengagement—they create value gaps that actual humans can't hope to successfully navigate.

Let's take a look at some common issues that arise in the context of families. I'm using family examples because we're all part of families. Even if we don't have children, we were raised by adults. In each case a significant gap has grown between the practiced values and the aspirational values, creating that dangerous disengagement divide.

1. Aspirational values: Honesty and Integrity

   Practiced values: Rationalizing and letting things slide

   Mom is always telling her kids that honesty and integrity are important, and that stealing and cheating in school won't be tolerated. As they pile into the car after a long grocery shop, Mom realizes that the cashier didn't charge her for the sodas in the bottom of the cart. Rather than going back into the store, she shrugs and says, "Wasn't my fault. They're making a mint anyway."

2. Aspirational values: Respect and Accountability

   Practiced value: Fast and easy is more important

   Dad is always driving home the importance of respect and accountability, but when Bobby intentionally breaks Sammy's new Transformer, Dad is too busy on his BlackBerry to sit down with the brothers and talk about how they should treat each other's toys. Instead of insisting that Bobby needs to apologize and make amends, he shrugs his shoulders, thinking, *Boys will be boys*, and tells them both to go to their rooms.

3. Aspirational values: Gratitude and Respect

   Practiced values: Teasing, taking for granted, disrespect

   Mom and Dad constantly feel underappreciated, and they're tired of their children's disrespectful attitudes. But Mom and Dad themselves yell at each other and call each other names. No one in the house says please or thank you, including the parents. Moreover, Mom and Dad use put-downs with their children and with each other, and everyone routinely teases family members to the point of tears. The problem is that the parents are looking for behaviors, emotions, and thinking patterns that their children have never seen modeled.

4. Aspirational Value: Setting Limits

    Practiced Values: Rebellion and cool are important

    Julie is seventeen and her younger brother, Austin, is fourteen. Julie and Austin's parents have a zero-tolerance policy for cigarettes, alcohol, and drugs. Unfortunately, that policy isn't working. Both kids have been caught smoking, and Julie has just been suspended because her teacher found vodka in her water bottle at school. Julie looks at her parents and screams, "You're such hypocrites! What about those wild parties y'all used to throw in high school? What about that time when Mom went to jail? Y'all thought that was so funny when you told us! You even showed us pictures."

Now, let's take a look at the power of aligned values:

1. Aspirational Values: Emotional Connection and Honored Feelings

    Practiced Values: Emotional Connection and Honored Feelings

Mom and Dad have tried to instill and model a "feelings first" ethic in their family. One evening Hunter comes home from basketball practice and is clearly upset. His sophomore year has been tough, and the basketball coach is really riding him. He throws his bag down on the kitchen floor and heads straight upstairs. Mom and Dad are in the kitchen making dinner, and they watch Hunter as he disappears up to his room. Dad turns off the burner, and Mom tells Hunter's younger brother that they're going to talk to Hunter and to please give them some time alone with him. They go upstairs together and sit on the edge of his bed. "Your mom and I know these past few weeks have been really hard," Dad says. "We don't know exactly how you feel, but we want to know. High school was tough for both of us, and we want to be with you in this." *This was such a great example of minding the gap and cultivating engagement! In the interview the father told me that it made all of them feel very vulnerable and that they were all crying before it was over. He said that sharing his high school struggles with his son really opened the relationship between them.*

I want to stress that these examples aren't fiction; they're from the data. And, no, we can't be perfect models all of the time. I know I can't. But when our practiced values are routinely in conflict with the expectations we set in our culture, disengagement is inevitable. If Mom is exhausted after the grocery shop and drives away without paying once, it might not be a big deal. If "I can get away with it and it's not my fault" is her norm, she needs to adjust her expectations around her kids' cheating. If she drives away without paying but then sits her kids down and says, "I should have gone back in and paid for the soda. It doesn't matter whose fault it was. I'm going back to the store today"—well, that's incredibly powerful. The lesson here is "I do want to live by my values and it's okay to be imperfect and make mistakes in this house. We just need to make it right when we can."

The example about the vodka illustrates a common struggle I hear from parents all of the time. "I was wild," they say. "I did things I don't want my kids to do. Should I lie about my escapades?" As a former wild person, I don't think the issue is whether to lie or not to lie. It's about what we share and *how* we share it. First, not everything we do or did is our children's business. Just as, when they're adults, not everything they do is our business. So we should examine the motivation for sharing a particular story and let the question about what we're teaching drive our decision. Second, having an honest talk with our kids about drugs and alcohol, and our experiences with either or both, can be helpful. But framing our numbing or party experiences as cool war stories and placing importance on being rebellious may eventually be at odds with the values we want our children to develop.

Remember the debate about culture and strategy? I think both are important and I think we need daring strategies to develop daring cultures. As these examples of aspirational values versus practiced values demonstrate, if we want to reconnect and reengage, we have to mind the gap.

Minding the gap is a daring strategy. We have to pay attention to the space between where we're actually standing and where we want to be. More importantly, we have to practice the values that we're holding out as important in our culture. Minding the gap requires both an embrace of our own vulnerability and cultivation of shame resilience—we're going to be called upon to show up as leaders and parents and educators in new and uncomfortable ways. We don't have to be perfect, just engaged and committed to aligning values with action. We also need to be prepared: The gremlins will be out in full force, as they love to sneak up just when we're about to step into the arena, be vulnerable, and take some chances.

In the next two chapters, I'm going to use the concepts I've introduced here to jump right in and tell you what I think we need to do both to cultivate engagement and to transform the way we parent, educate, and lead. These three questions will guide the following chapters:

1. How does the culture of "never enough" affect our schools, organizations, and families?
2. How do we recognize and combat shame at work, school, and home?
3. What does minding the gap and daring greatly look like in schools, organizations, and families?

CHAPTER 6
DISRUPTIVE ENGAGEMENT:
DARING TO REHUMANIZE EDUCATION AND WORK

To reignite creativity, innovation, and learning, leaders must rehumanize education and work. This means understanding how scarcity is affecting the way we lead and work, learning how to engage with vulnerability, and recognizing and combating shame. Make no mistake: honest conversations about vulnerability and shame are disruptive. The reason that we're not having these conversations in our organizations is that they shine light in dark corners. Once there is language, awareness, and understanding, turning back is almost impossible and carries with it severe consequences. We all want to dare greatly. If you give us a glimpse into that possibility, we'll hold on to it as our vision.

It can't be taken away.

Before we start this chapter, I want to clarify what I mean by "leader." I've come to believe that a leader is anyone who holds her- or himself accountable for finding potential in people and processes. The term leader has nothing to do with position, status, or number of direct reports. I wrote this chapter for all of us—parents, teachers, community volunteers, and CEOs—anyone who is willing to dare greatly and lead.

THE CHALLENGE OF LEADING IN A CULTURE OF "NEVER ENOUGH"

In 2010 I had the opportunity to spend a long weekend with fifty CEOs from Silicon Valley. One of the other speakers at the retreat was Kevin Surace, the then CEO of Serious Materials, and *Inc.* magazine's 2009 Entrepreneur of the Year. I knew Kevin was going to speak about disruptive innovation so in my first conversation with him, before either one of us had spoken to the group and before he knew about my work, I asked him this question: What's the most significant barrier to creativity and innovation?

Kevin thought about it for a minute and said, "I don't know if it has a name, but honestly, it's the fear of introducing an idea and being ridiculed, laughed at, and belittled. If you're willing to subject yourself to that experience, and if you survive it, then it becomes the fear of failure and the fear of being wrong. People believe they're only as good as their ideas and that their ideas can't seem too 'out there' and they can't 'not know' everything. The problem is that innovative ideas often sound crazy and failure and learning are part of revolution. Evolution and incremental change is important and we need it, but we're desperate for real revolution and that requires a different type of courage and creativity."

Before that conversation I had never specifically asked the leaders I'd interviewed about innovation, but everything Kevin was saying fit with my data on work and education. I smiled and responded, "It's true, isn't it? Most people and most organizations can't stand the uncertainty and the risk of real innovation. Learning and creating are inherently vulnerable. There's never enough certainty. People want guarantees."

He simply said, "Yes. Again, I'm not sure if there's a name for the problem, but something related to fear keeps people from going for it. They focus on what they already do well and they don't put themselves out there." There was a slight pause in our conversation before he looked at me and said, "So, I understand you're a researcher. What exactly do you do?"

I chuckled. "I study that *something related to fear*—I'm a shame-and-vulnerability researcher."

When I got back to my hotel room I grabbed my research journal and made notes about my conversation with Kevin. As I thought about that *something related to fear*, I remembered another set of notes that I had written in that same journal. I flipped back until I found the field notes that I had taken after talking to a group of middle school students about their classroom experiences. When I asked them to describe the key to learning, one girl gave the following reply while the others passionately nodded their heads and said, "Yes! That's it!" and "Exactly."

"There are times when you can ask questions or challenge ideas, but if you've got a teacher that doesn't like that or the kids in the class make fun of people who do that, it's bad. I think most of us learn that it's best to just keep your head down, your mouth shut, and your grades high."

As I reread this passage in my notes and thought about my conversation with Kevin, I was overwhelmed. As a teacher I felt heartbreak—we can't learn when our heads are down and our mouths are shut. As a mother of a middle school student and a kindergartener, I found it infuriating. As a researcher, it was the moment when I started to realize how often the struggles of our education system and the challenges we face in our workplaces mirror each other.

I first envisioned this as two separate discussions—one for educators and one for leaders. But as I looked back on the data, I realized that teachers and school administrators are leaders. C-level executives, managers, and supervisors are teachers. No corporation or school can thrive in the absence of creativity, innovation, and learning, and the greatest threat to all three of these is disengagement.

Given what I've learned from the research, and what I've observed over the past couple of years as I've worked with leaders from schools and companies of all sizes and types, I believe we have to completely reexamine the idea of engagement. **I call it disruptive engagement for this reason.** To reignite creativity, innovation, and learning, leaders must rehumanize education and work. This means understanding how scarcity is affecting the way we lead and work, learning how to engage with vulnerability, and recognizing and combating shame.

Sir Ken Robinson speaks to the power of making this shift in his appeal to leaders to replace the outdated idea that human organizations should work like machines with a metaphor that captures the realities of humanity. In his book *Out of Our Minds: Learning to be Creative*, Robinson writes, "However seductive the machine metaphor may be for industrial production, human organizations are not actually mechanisms and people are not components in them. People have values and feelings, perceptions, opinions, motivations, and biographies, whereas cogs and sprockets do not. An organization is not the physical facilities within which it operates; it is the networks of people in it."

Make no mistake: Rehumanizing work and education requires courageous leadership. Honest conversations about vulnerability and shame are disruptive. The reason that we're not having these conversations in our organizations is that they shine light in the dark corners. Once there is language, awareness, and understanding, turning back is almost impossible and carries with it severe consequences. We all want to Dare Greatly. If you give us a glimpse into that possibility, we'll hold on to it as our vision. It can't be taken away.

RECOGNIZING AND COMBATING SHAME

Shame breeds fear. It crushes our tolerance for vulnerability, thereby killing engagement, innovation, creativity, productivity, and trust. And worst of all, if we don't know what we're looking for, shame can ravage our organizations before we see one outward sign of a problem. Shame works like termites in a house. It's hidden in the dark behind the walls and constantly eating away at our infrastructure, until one day the stairs suddenly crumble. Only then do we realize that it's only a matter of time before the walls come tumbling down.

In the same way that a casual walk around our house won't reveal a termite problem, a stroll through an office or a school won't necessarily reveal a shame problem. Or at least we hope it's not that obvious. If it is—if we see a manager berating an employee or a teacher shaming a student—the problem is already acute and more than likely has been happening for a long time. In most cases, though, we have to know what we're looking for when we assess an organization for signs that shame may be an issue.

SIGNS THAT SHAME HAS PERMEATED THE CULTURE

Blaming, gossiping, favoritism, name-calling, and harassment are all behavior cues that shame has permeated a culture. A more obvious sign is when shame becomes an outright management tool. Is there evidence of people in leadership roles bullying others, criticizing subordinates in front of colleagues, delivering public reprimands, or setting up reward systems that intentionally belittle, shame, or humiliate people?

I've never been to a shame-free school or organization. I'm not saying it doesn't exist, but I doubt it. In fact, once I've explained how shame works, I normally have one or two teachers approach me and explain that they use shame on a daily basis. Most ask how to change that practice, but a few proudly say, "It works." The best-case scenario is that it's a limited or contained problem, rather than a cultural norm. One reason that I'm confident that shame exists in schools is simply because 85 percent of the men and women we interviewed for the shame research could recall a school incident from their childhood that was so shaming, it changed how they thought of themselves as learners. What makes this even more haunting is that approximately half of those recollections were what I refer to as creativity scars. The research participants could point to a specific incident where they were told or shown that they weren't good writers, artists, musicians, dancers, or something creative. I still see this happening in schools all of the time. Art is graded on narrow standards and kids as young as kindergarten are told they have creative gifts. This helps explain why the gremlins are so powerful when it comes to creativity and innovation.

Corporations have their own struggles. The Workplace Bullying Institute (WBI) defines bullying as "Repeated mistreatment: sabotage by others that prevented work from getting done, verbal abuse, threatening conduct, intimidation, and humiliation." A 2010 poll conducted by Zogby International for WBI reported that an estimated 54 million American workers (37 percent of the US workforce) have been bullied at work. Furthermore, another WBI report revealed that 52.5 percent of the time, bullied workers reported that employers basically did nothing to stop the bullying.

When we see shame being used as a management tool (again, that means bullying, criticism in front of colleagues, public reprimands, or reward systems that intentionally belittle people), we need to take direct action because it means that we've got an infestation on our hands. And we need to remember that this doesn't just happen overnight. Equally important to keep in mind is that shame is like the other "sh" word. Like shit, shame rolls downhill. If employees are constantly having to navigate shame, you can bet that they're passing it on to their customers, students, and families.

So, if it's happening and it can be isolated to a specific unit, work team, or person, it has to be addressed immediately *and without shame*. We learn shame in our families of origin, and many people grow up believing that it's an effective and efficient way to manage people, run a classroom, and parent. For that reason, shaming someone who's using shame is not helpful. But doing nothing is equally dangerous, not only for the people who are targets of the shaming but also for the entire organization.

Several years ago a man came up to me after an event and said, "Interview me! Please! I'm a financial advisor and you wouldn't believe what happens in my office." When I met Don for the interview, he told me that in his organization you choose your office each quarter based on your quarterly results: The person with the best results chooses first and sends the person in the desired office packing.

He shook his head, and his voice cracked a bit when he said, "Given that I've had the best numbers for the past six quarters, you'd think I'd like that. But I don't. I absolutely hate it. It's a miserable environment." He then told me how after the previous quarterly results were in, his boss walked into his office, closed the door, and told him that he had to move offices.

"At first I thought my numbers had dropped. Then he told me that he didn't care if I had the best numbers or if I liked my office; the point was to terrorize the other guys. He said, 'Busting their balls in public builds character. It's motivating.'"

Before the end of our interview, he told me he was job hunting. "I'm good at my job and even enjoy it, but I didn't sign up to terrorize people. I never knew why it felt so shitty, but after hearing you talk, now I do. It's shame. It's worse than high school. I'll find a better place to work, and you can be damn sure that I'm taking my clients with me."

In *I Thought It Was Just Me*, I tell the following story about Sylvia, an event planner in her thirties who jumped right into our interview by saying, "I wish you could have interviewed me six months ago. I was a different person. I was so stuck in shame." When I asked her what she meant, she explained that she had heard about my research from a friend and volunteered to be interviewed because she felt her life had been changed by shame. She had recently had an important breakthrough when she found herself on the "losers' list" at work.

Apparently, after two years of what her employer called "outstanding, winners' work," she had made her first big mistake. The mistake cost her agency a major client. Her boss's response was to put her on the "losers' list." She said, "In one minute I went from being on the winners' board to being at the top of the losers' list." I guess I must have winced when Sylvia referred to the "losers' list" because, without my remarking at all, she said, "I know, it's terrible. My boss has these two big dry-erase boards outside of his office. One's the winners' list, and one board is for the losers." She said for weeks she could barely function. She lost her confidence and started missing work. Shame, anxiety, and fear took over. After a difficult three-week period, she quit her job and went to work for another agency.

Shame can only rise so far in any system before people disengage to protect themselves. When we're disengaged, we don't show up, we don't contribute, and we stop caring. On the far end of the spectrum, disengagement allows people to rationalize all kinds of unethical behavior including lying, stealing, and cheating. In the case of Don and Sylvia, they didn't just disengage; they quit and took their talent to competitors.

As we assess our organizations for signs of shame, it's also important to be aware of external threats—forces outside of our organizations that are influencing how both leaders and employees feel about their work. As a teacher, the sister of two public school teachers, and the sister-in-law of a public high school vice-principal, I don't have to look far for examples of this.

Several years ago my sister Ashley called me crying. When I asked her what was wrong, she told me that the *Houston Chronicle* had published the name of every schoolteacher in the Houston Independent School District along with the bonus they received based on their students' standardized test scores. I hadn't seen the paper that day and I was stunned. And I was also confused.

"Ashley, you teach kindergarten. Your kids don't take the tests yet. Is your name in there?"

Ashley explained that her name was in there and that the paper reported that she got the lowest bonus available. What they didn't report was that it was the highest bonus available to kindergarten teachers. Imagine doing that—reporting everyone's salaries or bonuses and moreover reporting them inaccurately—to any other group of professionals.

"I'm in a total shame meltdown," Ashley said, still crying. "All I've ever wanted to do was to be a teacher. I work my butt off. I've hit up everyone in our family for money so I can buy school supplies for the kids who can't afford them. I stay after and help the parents help their kids. I don't get it. There are hundreds of teachers like me, and do you read about that in the paper? No. And it's not just about me. Some of the very best teachers I know volunteer to teach some of the most challenging students without any thought about how it's going to affect their scores or bonuses. They do it because they love their work and they believe in the kids."

Unfortunately, the "Scarlet Letter" approach to teacher evaluation is not just happening in Texas—it's become an accepted practice across the nation. The good news is that people are finally daring greatly and speaking up. In response to the New York State Court of Appeals ruling that teachers' individual performance assessments could be made public, Bill Gates wrote this in a *New York Times* op-ed: "Developing a systematic way to help teachers get better is the most powerful idea in education today. The surest way to weaken it is to twist it into a capricious exercise in public shaming. Let's focus on creating a personnel system that truly helps teachers improve."

When I posted Gates's op-ed on my Facebook page, many teachers left comments. I was moved by this response from a veteran teacher: "For me, teaching is about love. It is not about transferring information, but rather creating an atmosphere of mystery and imagination and discovery. When I begin to lose myself because of some unresolved pain or fears or the overpowering feelings of shame, then I no longer teach . . . I deliver information and I think I become irrelevant then."

Teachers are not the only ones who wrestle with shame delivered (usually in the public media) from outside of the organization. I'm often asked to address this issue when I'm speaking with professionals who are routinely vilified, disliked, or misunderstood by the public—lawyers, dentists, and folks from the financial industry are a few. We might roll our eyes and think, *C'mon, we love to hate them!* But I can tell you from my experiences that it's not fun to feel hated simply for doing work that means something to you, and it can take a serious toll on individuals and cultures.

As leaders, the most effective thing we can do when this

kind of media abuse is happening is speak out, insist on accuracy and accountability, and confront it head on with the people affected by it. We can't pretend that it's not hurting our employees. On a personal level, we can resist buying into and perpetuating the public stereotyping of professions that by their nature operate in realms of personal stress.

THE BLAME GAME

Here's the best way to think about the relationship between shame and blame: If blame is driving, shame is riding shotgun. In organizations, schools, and families, blaming and finger-pointing are often symptoms of shame. Shame researchers June Tangney and Ronda Dearing explain that in shame-bound relationships, people "measure carefully, weigh, and assign blame." They write, "In the face of any negative outcome, large or small, *someone* or *something* must be found responsible (and held accountable). There's no notion of 'water under the bridge.'" They go on to say, "After all, if *someone* must be to blame and it's not me, it must be you! From blame comes shame. And then hurt, denial, anger, and retaliation."

Blame is simply the discharging of pain and discomfort. We blame when we're uncomfortable and experience pain—when we're vulnerable, angry, hurt, in shame, grieving. There's nothing productive about blame, and it often involves shaming someone or just being mean. If blame is a pattern in your culture, then shame needs to be addressed as an issue.

COVER-UP CULTURE

Related to blame is the issue of cover-ups. Just like blame is a sign of shame-based organizations, cover-up cultures depend on shame to keep folks quiet. When the culture of an organization mandates that it is more important to protect the reputation of a system and those in power than it is to protect the basic human dignity of individuals or communities, you can be certain that shame is systemic, money drives ethics, and accountability is dead. This is true in all systems, from corporations, nonprofits, universities, and governments, to churches, schools, families, and sports programs. If you think back on any major incidents fueled by cover-ups, you'll see this pattern.

In an organizational culture where respect and the dignity of individuals are held as the highest values, shame and blame don't work as management styles. There is no leading by fear. Empathy is a valued asset, accountability is an expectation rather than an exception, and the primal human need for belonging is not used as leverage and social control. We can't control the behavior of individuals; however, we can cultivate organizational cultures where behaviors are not tolerated and people are held accountable for protecting what matters most: human beings.

We won't solve the complex issues that we're facing today without creativity, innovation, and engaged learning. We can't afford to let our discomfort with the topic of shame get in the way of recognizing and combating it in our schools and workplaces. The four best strategies for building shame-resilient organizations are:

1. Supporting leaders who are willing to dare greatly and facilitate honest conversations about shame and cultivate shame-resilient cultures.
2. Facilitating a conscientious effort to see where shame might be functioning in the organization and how it might even be creeping into

the way we engage with our co-workers and students.

3. Normalizing is a critical shame-resilience strategy. Leaders and managers can cultivate engagement by helping people know what to expect. What are common struggles? How have other people dealt with them? What have your experiences been?

4. Training all employees on the differences between shame and guilt, and teaching them how to give and receive feedback in a way that fosters growth and engagement.

MINDING THE GAP WITH FEEDBACK

A *daring greatly* culture is a culture of honest, constructive, and engaged feedback. This is true in organizations, schools, and families. I know families struggle with this issue; however, I was shocked to see "lack of feedback" emerge as a primary concern in the interviews that focused on work experiences. Today's organizations are so metric-focused in their evaluation of performance that giving, receiving, and soliciting valuable feedback ironically has become rare. It's even a rarity in schools where learning depends on feedback, which is infinitely more effective than grades scribbled on the top of a page or computer-generated, standardized test scores.

The problem is straightforward: Without feedback there can be no transformative change. When we don't talk to the people we're leading about their strengths and their opportunities for growth, they begin to question their contributions and our commitment. Disengagement follows.

When I asked people why there was such a lack of feedback in their organizations and schools, they used different language, but the two major issues were the same:

1. We're not comfortable with hard conversations.
2. We don't know how to give and receive feedback in a way that moves people and processes forward.

The good news is that these are very fixable problems. If an organization makes the creation of a feedback culture a priority and a practice, rather than an aspirational value, it can happen. People are desperate for feedback—we all want to grow. We just need to learn how to give feedback in a way that inspires growth and engagement.

Right off the bat, I believe that feedback thrives in cultures where the goal is not "getting comfortable with hard conversations" but *normalizing discomfort*. If leaders expect real learning, critical thinking, and change, then discomfort should be normalized: "We believe growth and learning are uncomfortable so it's going to happen here—you're going to feel that way. We want you to know that it's normal and it's an expectation here. You're not alone and we ask that you stay open and lean into it." This is true at all levels and in all organizations, schools, faith communities, and even families. I've observed this pattern of normalized discomfort in the Wholehearted organizations I've researched and I've lived it in my classroom and with my family.

I learned to teach by immersing myself in books on engaged and critical pedagogy by writers like bell hooks and Paulo Freire. At first, I was terrified by the idea that if education is going to be transformative, it's going to be uncomfortable and unpredictable. Now, as I begin my fifteenth year of teaching at the University of Houston, I always tell my students, "If you're comfortable, I'm not teaching and you're not learning. It's going to get uncomfortable in here and that's okay. It's normal and it's part of the process."

The simple and honest process of letting people know that discomfort is normal, it's going to happen, why it happens, and why it's important, reduces anxiety, fear, and shame. Periods of discomfort become an expectation and a norm. In fact, most semesters I have students who approach me after class and say, "I haven't been uncomfortable yet. I'm concerned." These exchanges often lead to critically important conversations and feedback about their engagement and my teaching. The big challenge for leaders is getting our heads and hearts around the fact that we need to cultivate the courage to be uncomfortable and to teach the people around us how to accept discomfort as a part of growth.

For the best guidance on how to give feedback that moves people and processes forward, I turn to my social work roots. In my experience the heart of valuable feedback is taking the "strengths perspective." According to social work educator Dennis Saleebey, viewing performance from the strengths perspective offers us the opportunity to examine our struggles in light of our capacities, talents, competencies, possibilities, visions, values, and hopes. This perspective doesn't dismiss the serious nature of our struggles; however, it does require us to consider our positive qualities as potential resources. Dr. Saleebey proposes, "It is as wrong to deny the possible as it is to deny the problem."

One effective method for understanding our strengths is to examine the relationship between strengths and limitations. If we look at what we do best as well as what we want to change the most, we will often find that the two are varying degrees of the same core behavior. Most of us can go through the majority of our "faults" or "limitations" and find strengths lurking within.

For example, I can beat myself up for being too controlling and micromanaging, or I can recognize that I'm very responsible, dependable, and committed to quality work. The micromanaging issues don't go away, but by viewing them from a strengths perspective, I have the confidence to look at myself and assess the behaviors I'd like to change.

I want to emphasize that the strengths perspective is not a tool to simply allow us to put a positive spin on a problem and consider it solved. But by first enabling us to inventory our strengths, it suggests ways we can use those strengths to address the related challenges. One way I teach this perspective to students is by requiring them to give and receive feedback on their classroom presentations. When a student presents, s/he receives feedback from every one of his or her classmates. The students in the audience have to identify three observable strengths and one opportunity for growth. The trick is that they have to use their assessment of the strengths to make a suggestion on how the individual might address the specified opportunity. For example:

Strengths

1. You captured my interest right away with your emotional personal story.
2. You used examples that are relevant to my life.
3. You concluded with actionable strategies that tied in with our learning in the class.

Opportunity

> Your stories and examples made me feel con-
> nected to you and what you were saying, but I
> sometimes struggled to read the PowerPoint
> and listen to you at the same time. I didn't want
> to miss anything you were saying, but I worried
> about not following the slides. You might ex-
> periment with fewer words on the slides—or
> maybe even no slides. You had me without them.

The research has made this clear: **Vulnerability is at the heart of the feedback process.** This is true whether we give, receive, or solicit feedback. And the vulnerability doesn't go away even if we're trained and experienced in offering and getting feedback. Experience does, however, give us the ad-vantage of knowing that we can survive the exposure and un-certainty, and that it's worth the risk.

One of the greatest mistakes that I see people make in the feedback process is "armoring up." To protect ourselves from the vulnerability of giving or receiving feedback, we get ready to rumble (cue *Jock Jams*). It's easy to assume that the feedback process only feels vulnerable for the person receiving the feed-back, but that's not true. Honest engagement around expecta-tions and behavior is always fraught with uncertainty, risk, and emotional exposure for everyone involved. Here's an example. Susan, the principal of a large high school, has to talk to one of her teachers about several parent complaints. The parents have voiced concerns about the teacher's cursing during class and making personal calls on her cell phone while she allows her students to leave the class, goof off, and make their own calls. In this situation "armoring up" can take several forms.

One is that Susan can fill out the probation form and have it sitting on her desk when the teacher comes in. She'll simply say, "Here's the complaint. I've written you up for the following offenses. Sign here and don't let it happen again." She's knocked out the meeting in three minutes flat. There's no feedback, no growth, no learning, but it's over. The odds of the teacher changing her behaviors are slim.

Another way we armor up is by convincing ourselves that the other person deserves to be hurt or put down. Like most of us, Susan is more comfortable with anger than vulnerability, so she ratchets up her confidence with a little self-righteousness. "I'm so sick of this. If these teachers respected me, they'd never do stuff like this. I've had it. She's been a problem since the first day I met her. *You want to jack around in class—go for it. I'll show you exactly how this works.*" The opportunity for constructive feedback and relationship building turns into a smackdown. Again, it's over but there is no feedback, no growth, no learning and, more than likely, no change.

I'll admit that I've got a lot of "bring it on" in me. I'm scrappy, I think fast on my feet, and I like my emotions with a little agency. I'm good at anger and only so-so at vulnerability, so armoring up before a vulnerable experience is attractive to me. Luckily, this work has taught me that when I feel self-righteous, it means I'm afraid. It's a way to puff up and protect myself when I'm afraid of being wrong, making someone angry, or getting blamed.

SITTING ON THE SAME SIDE OF THE TABLE

In my social work training, a lot of attention was paid to how we talk to people, even down to where and how we sit. For example, I would never talk to a client across a desk; I would walk around my desk and sit in a chair across from the client so there was nothing big and bulky between us. I remember the first time I went in to see one of my social work professors about a grade. She got up from behind her desk and asked me to take a seat at a small round table she had in her office. She pulled up a chair and sat next to me.

In armoring up for that conversation, I had pictured her sitting behind her big metal desk and me defiantly sliding my paper across it and demanding an explanation for my grade. After she sat down next to me, I put the paper on the table. As she said, "I'm so glad that you came in to talk to me about your paper. You did a great job on this; I loved your conclusion," and patted me on the back, I awkwardly realized that we were on the same side of the table.

Totally discombobulated, I blurted, "Thank you. I worked really hard on it."

She nodded and said, "I can tell. Thank you. I took some points off for your APA formatting. I'd like for you to focus on that and get it cleaned up. You could submit this for publication, and I don't want the reference formatting to hold you back."

I was still confused. *She thinks it's publishable? She liked it?*

"Do you need some help with the APA formatting? It's tricky and it took me years to get it down," she asked. (*A great example of normalizing.*)

· I told her that I'd fix the references and I asked her if she'd look at my revisions. She happily agreed and gave me a few tips on the process. I thanked her for her time and left, grateful for my grade and for a teacher who cared as much as she did.

Today, "Sitting on the same side of the table" is my metaphor for feedback. I used it to create my *Engaged Feedback Checklist:*

I know I'm ready to give feedback when:

I'm ready to sit next to you rather than across from you;

I'm willing to put the problem in front of us rather than between us (or sliding it toward you);

I'm ready to listen, ask questions, and accept that I may not fully understand the issue;

I want to acknowledge what you do well instead of picking apart your mistakes;

I recognize your strengths and how you can use them to address your challenges;

I can hold you accountable without shaming or blaming you;

I'm willing to own my part;

I can genuinely thank you for your efforts rather than criticize you for your failings;

I can talk about how resolving these challenges will lead to your growth and opportunity; and

I can model the vulnerability and openness that I expect to see from you.

You can find a printed copy of this checklist on my website (www.brene brown.com).

How would education be different if students, teachers, and parents sat on the same side of the table? How would engagement change if leaders sat down next to folks and said, "Thank you for your contributions. Here's how you're making a difference. This issue is getting in the way of your growth, and I think we can tackle it together. What ideas do you have about moving forward? What role do you think I'm playing in the problem? What can I do differently to support you?"

Let's go back to the example with Susan, the principal who was armoring up for a smackdown. If she read through this checklist she'd realize that she's not in a place to give feedback, to be a leader. But with parenting complaints stacking up on her desk, time is an issue for her and she knows the situation needs to be addressed. It can be very difficult to move into the right head and heart space to give feedback when we're under pressure.

So, how do we create a safe space for vulnerability and growth when we're not feeling open? Armored feedback doesn't facilitate lasting and meaningful change—I don't know a single person who can be open to accepting feedback or owning responsibility for something when they're being hammered. Our hardwiring takes over and we self-protect.

Susan's best bet is to model the openness that she hopes to see, and solicit feedback from one of her colleagues. When I interviewed participants who valued feedback and worked at it, they talked about the necessity of soliciting feedback from their peers, asking for advice, and even role-playing difficult situations. If we're not willing to ask for feedback and receive it, we'll never be good at giving it. If Susan can work through her own feelings so that she can be present with her employee, she's much more likely to see the change that she's requesting.

Some of you might be wondering, "Susan's employee problem is pretty straightforward and small. Why would she need to spend time soliciting feedback from one of her colleagues for a problem like that?" It's a good question with an important answer: The size, severity, or complexity of a problem doesn't always reflect our emotional reactivity to it. If Susan can't get to the same side of the table with this teacher, it doesn't matter how simple the problem is or how clear the violation is. What Susan might learn from her peer is that she's really triggered by this particular teacher or that she's armoring up because unprofessional behavior is becoming a dangerous norm among this cluster of teachers. Giving and soliciting feedback is about learning and growth, and understanding who we are and how we respond to the people around us is the foundation in this process.

Again, there's no question that feedback may be one of the most difficult arenas to negotiate in our lives. We should remember, though, that victory is not getting good feedback, avoiding giving difficult feedback, or avoiding the need for feedback. Instead it's taking off the armor, showing up, and engaging.

THE COURAGE TO BE VULNERABLE

I recently gave a talk at the University of Houston's Wolff Center for Entrepreneurship. The program, which pairs thirty-five to forty elite undergraduate students with mentors and offers comprehensive business training, is ranked as the leading undergrad entrepreneurship program in the United States. I was asked to talk to the students about vulnerability and the power of story.

During the Q&A session after my talk, one of the students asked me a question that I'm sure is often on the minds of people when I talk about vulnerability. He said, "I can see how vulnerability is important, but I'm in sales and I don't get what that looks like. Does being vulnerable mean that if a customer asks me a question about a product and I don't know the answer, I just say what I'm thinking: 'I'm new and I really don't know what I'm doing?'"

The students, who were all turned around listening to him, turned back in their chairs and looked at me as if to say, "Yeah, that seems lame. Are we really supposed to do that?"

My answer was no. And yes. In that scenario vulnerability is recognizing and owning that you don't know something; it's looking the customer in the eye and saying, "I don't know the answer to that, but I'll find out. I want to make sure you have the correct information." I explained that the unwillingness to engage with the vulnerability of not knowing often leads to making excuses, dodging the question, or—worst-case scenario—bullshitting. That's the deathblow in any relationship, and the one thing I've learned from talking to people who sell for a living is that sales is all about relationships.

So, while I wouldn't take that tack with the customer, I do think there's some value in sharing the feeling of not knowing what you're doing with *someone*—whether a mentor who can offer support and guidance or a colleague who can help you learn and normalize your experience. Imagine the stress and anxiety of not knowing what you're doing, trying to convince a customer that you do, not being able to ask for help, and not having anyone to talk to about your struggle. This is how we lose people. It's too difficult to stay engaged in these circumstances. We start cutting corners, we stop caring, and we check out. After my talk, one of the mentors came up to me and said, "I've been in sales my entire career, and let me tell you, there's nothing more important than having the courage to say, 'I don't know,' and 'I messed up'—being honest and open is key to success in every part of our lives."

Last year I had the opportunity to interview Gay Gaddis, the owner and founder of T3 (The Think Tank) in Austin,

Texas. T3 is a top integrated marketing firm that specializes in innovative marketing campaigns that cut across all media. In 1989, Gay cashed in a sixteen-thousand-dollar IRA with the dream of starting an advertising agency. Twenty-three years after opening with a handful of regional accounts, Gay has built T3 into the nation's largest advertising agency wholly owned by a woman. With offices in Austin, New York, and San Francisco, T3 works with clients including Microsoft, UPS, JPMorgan Chase, Pfizer, Allstate, Coca-Cola, and Sprite. Her dynamic business acumen and corporate culture have led to national recognition. She has been named one of *Fast Company*'s Top 25 Women Business Builders, *Inc.* magazine's Top 10 Entrepreneurs of the Year, and one of the top 25 Advertising Working Mothers of the Year by *Working Mother* magazine. Gay and T3's family-friendly workplace program, "T3 and Under," was even recognized by the White House.

I jumped right into my interview with Gay by telling her that a business journalist had recently told me that, unlike leaders in corporations who are shielded by layers of systems, entrepreneurs can't afford to be vulnerable. When I asked her what she thought about that proposition, she smiled. "When you shut down vulnerability, you shut down opportunity."

Here's how she explained it: "By definition, entrepreneurship is vulnerable. It's all about the ability to handle and manage uncertainty. People are constantly changing, budgets change, boards change, and competition means you have to stay nimble and innovative. You have to create a vision and live up to that vision. There is no vision without vulnerability."

Knowing that Gay spends a considerable amount of time teaching and mentoring, I asked her what advice she gives new entrepreneurs about embracing uncertainty. She said,

"Success requires entrepreneurs to cultivate strong support networks and good mentors. You need to learn how to shut out the noise so you can get clear on how you feel and what you think, and then you do the hard work. No question—it's all about vulnerability."

Another great example of the power of vulnerability—this time in a corporation—is the leadership approach taken by Lululemon's CEO, Christine Day. In a video interview with CNN Money, Day explained that she was once a very bright, smart executive who "majored in being right." Her transformation came when she realized that getting people to engage and take ownership wasn't about "the telling" but about letting them come into the idea in a purpose-led way, and that her job was creating the space for others to perform. She characterized this change as the shift from "having the best idea or problem solving" to "being the best leader of people."

The shift she described is the shift from controlling to engaging with vulnerability—taking risks and cultivating trust. And while vulnerability can sometimes make us feel powerless, her shift was a total power move. Day has increased the number of stores from 71 to 174, while total revenue has grown from $297 million to almost $1 billion, and Lululemon's stock is up about 300 percent since its 2007 IPO.

In a written interview with Day accompanying the video, the idea of vulnerability as the birthplace of creativity, innovation, and trust continued to play out—even when it comes to failure and defeat. One of Day's leadership guideposts is "finding the magic makers." As Day explained, "Taking responsibility, taking risks, and having an entrepreneurial spirit are qualities we look for in our employees. We want people who bring their own magic. Athletes are great within our culture; they're used to winning as well as losing. They know how to handle—and fix—defeat." Day also emphasized the importance of allowing people to make mistakes: "Our golden rule? If you screw up, you clean it up."

In businesses, schools, faith communities—any system, even families—we can tell a lot about how people engage with vulnerability by observing how often and how openly you hear people saying:

- I don't know.
- I need help.
- I'd like to give it a shot.
- It's important to me.
- I disagree—can we talk about it?
- It didn't work, but I learned a lot.
- Yes, I did it.
- Here's what I need.
- Here's how I feel.
- I'd like some feedback.
- Can I get your take on this?
- What can I do better next time?
- Can you teach me how to do this?
- I played a part in that.
- I accept responsibility for that.
- I'm here for you.

> - I want to help.
>
> - Let's move on.
>
> - I'm sorry.
>
> - That means a lot to me.
>
> - Thank you.

For leaders, vulnerability often looks and feels like discomfort. In his book *Tribes: We Need You to Lead Us*, Seth Godin writes, "Leadership is scarce because few people are willing to go through the discomfort required to lead. This scarcity makes leadership valuable. . . . It's uncomfortable to stand up in front of strangers. It's uncomfortable to propose an idea that might fail. It's uncomfortable to challenge the status quo. It's uncomfortable to resist the urge to settle. When you identify the discomfort, you've found the place where a leader is needed. If you're not uncomfortable in your work as a leader, it's almost certain you're not reaching your potential as a leader."

As I looked over the data and read through my notes from the interviews I've done with leaders, I wondered what students would say to teachers and what teachers would say to their principals if they had the opportunity to ask for the leadership they needed. I wondered what the customer service representative would say to his boss and what she might ask of her boss. What do we want people to know about us and what do we need from them?

As I started writing down the answers to these questions, I realized that they sounded like a mandate; a manifesto. Here's what emerged from these questions:

The Daring Greatly
Leadership Manifesto

To the CEOs and teachers. To the principals and the managers. To the politicians, community leaders, and decision-makers:

We want to show up, we want to learn, and we want to inspire.

We are hardwired for connection, curiosity, and engagement.

We crave purpose, and we have a deep desire to create and contribute.

We want to take risks, embrace our vulnerabilities, and be courageous.

When learning and working are dehumanized—when you no longer see us and no longer encourage our daring, or when you only see what we produce or how we perform—we disengage and turn away from the very things that the world needs from us: our talent, our ideas, and our passion.

What we ask is that you engage with us, show up beside us, and learn from us.

Feedback is a function of respect; when you don't have honest conversations with us about our strengths and our opportunities for growth, we question our contributions and your commitment.

Above all else, we ask that you show up, let yourself be seen, and be courageous. Dare Greatly with us.

You can find a printed copy of this manifesto on my website (www.brene brown.com).

CHAPTER 7
WHOLEHEARTED PARENTING:
DARING TO BE THE ADULTS
WE WANT OUR CHILDREN TO BE

Who we are and how we engage with the world are much stronger predictors of how our children will do than what we know about parenting. In terms of teaching our children to dare greatly in the "never enough" culture, the question isn't so much "Are you parenting the right way?" as it is: "Are you the adult that you want your child to grow up to be?"

PARENTING IN A CULTURE OF NEVER ENOUGH

Most of us would love a color-coded parenting handbook that answers all of our unanswerable questions, comes with guarantees, and minimizes our vulnerability. We want to know that if we follow certain rules or adhere to the method espoused by a certain parenting expert, our children will sleep through the night, be happy, make friends, achieve professional success, and stay safe. The uncertainty of parenting can bring up feelings in us that range from frustration to terror.

Our need for certainty in an endeavor as uncertain as raising children makes explicit "how-to-parent" strategies both seductive and dangerous. I say "dangerous" because certainty often breeds absolutes, intolerance, and judgment. That's why parents are so critical of one another—we latch on to a method or approach and very quickly *our* way becomes *the* way. When we obsess over our parenting choices to the extent that most of us do, and then see someone else making different choices, we often perceive that difference as direct criticism of how we are parenting.

Ironically, parenting is a shame and judgment minefield precisely *because* most of us are wading through uncertainty and self-doubt when it comes to raising our children. After all, we rarely engage in self-righteous judgment when we feel confident about our decisions: I'm not going to practically knock myself unconscious with a shaming eye roll about your nonorganic milk if I feel good about what I'm feeding my children. But if doubt lurks beneath my choices, that self-righteous critic will spring to life in not-so-subtle parenting moments that happen because my underlying fear of not being *the perfect parent* is driving my need to confirm that, at the very least, *I'm better than you.*

Somewhere buried deep inside our hopes and fears for our children is the terrifying truth that there is no such thing as perfect parenting and there are no guarantees. From debates about attachment parenting and how much better they parent in Europe to disparagement of "tiger moms" and helicopter parents, the heated discussions that occupy much of the national parenting conversation conveniently distract us from this important and difficult truth: Who we are and how we engage with the world are much stronger predictors of how our children will do than what we know about parenting.

I'm not a parenting expert. In fact, I'm not sure that I even believe in the idea of "parenting experts." I'm an engaged, imperfect parent and a passionate researcher. As I mentioned in the introduction, I'm an experienced mapmaker and a stumbling traveler. Like many of you, parenting is by far my boldest and most daring adventure.

From the very beginning of my research on shame, I've always collected data on parenting and paid close attention to how research participants talked about being parented and about parenting. The reason is simple: Our stories of worthiness—of being enough—begin in our first families. The narrative certainly doesn't end there, but what we learn about ourselves and how we learn to engage with the world as children sets a course that either will require us to spend a significant part of our life fighting to reclaim our self-worth or will give us hope, courage, and resilience for our journey.

There's no question that our behavior, thinking, and emotions are both hardwired within us and influenced by our environment. I wouldn't hazard a guess on the percentages, and I'm convinced that we'll never have a precise nature/nurture breakdown. I have no doubt, however, that when it comes to our sense of love, belonging, and worthiness, we are most radically shaped by our families of origin—what we hear, what we are told, and perhaps most importantly, how we observe our parents engaging with the world.

As parents, we may have less control than we *think* over temperament and personality, and less control than we *want* over the scarcity culture. But we do have powerful parenting opportunities in other areas: how we help our children understand, leverage, and appreciate their hardwiring, and how we teach them resilience in the face of relentless "never enough" cultural messages. In terms of teaching our children to dare greatly in the "never enough" culture, the question isn't so much "Are you parenting the right way?" as it is: "Are you the adult that you want your child to grow up to be?"

As Joseph Chilton Pearce writes, "What we *are* teaches the child more than what we say, so we must *be* what we want our children to become." Even though the vulnerability of parenting is terrifying at times, we can't afford to armor ourselves against it or push it away—it is our richest, most fertile ground for teaching and cultivating connection, meaning, and love.

Vulnerability lies at the center of the family story. It defines our moments of greatest joy, fear, sorrow, shame, disappointment, love, belonging, gratitude, creativity, and everyday wonder. Whether we're holding our children or standing beside them or chasing them down or talking through their locked door, vulnerability is what shapes who we are and who our children are.

By pushing away vulnerability, we turn parenting into a competition that's about knowing, proving, executing, and measuring rather than *being*. If we put aside the question of "Who's better?" and put down the yardsticks of school admissions, grades, sports, trophies, and accomplishments, I think the vast majority of us will agree that what we want for our children is what we want for ourselves—we want to raise children who live and love with their whole hearts.

If Wholeheartedness is the goal, then above all else we should strive to raise children who:

- Engage with the world from a place of worthiness

- Embrace their vulnerabilities and imperfections

- Feel a deep sense of love and compassion for themselves and others

- Value hard work, perseverance, and respect

- Carry a sense of authenticity and belonging with them, rather than searching for it in external places

- Have the courage to be imperfect, vulnerable, and creative

- Don't fear feeling ashamed or unlovable if they are different or if they are struggling

- Move through our rapidly changing world with courage and a resilient spirit

For parents this means we are called upon to:

- Acknowledge that we can't give our children what we don't have and so we must let them share in our journey to grow, change, and learn

- Recognize our own armor and model for our children how to take it off, be vulnerable, show up, and let ourselves be seen and known

- Honor our children by continuing on our own journeys toward Wholeheartedness

- Parent from a place of "enough" rather than scarcity

- Mind the gap and practice the values we want to teach

- Dare greatly, possibly more than we've ever dared before

In other words, if we want our children to love and accept who they are, our job is to love and accept who *we* are. We can't use fear, shame, blame, and judgment in our own lives if we want to raise courageous children. Compassion and connection—the very things that give purpose and meaning to our lives—can only be learned if they are experienced. And our families are our first opportunities to experience these things.

In this chapter, I want to share what I've learned about worthiness, shame resilience, and vulnerability specifically from my parenting research. This work has profoundly transformed the way that Steve and I think and feel about parenting. It has dramatically changed our priorities, our marriage, and our day-to-day behaviors. Because Steve is a pediatrician, we spend lots of time discussing parenting research and various parenting models. My goal here is not to teach you how to parent, but to share what might be a new lens through which to view the great dare of raising Wholehearted children.

UNDERSTANDING AND COMBATING SHAME

It's a terrible myth to believe that once we have children, our journey ends and theirs begins. For many of us, the most interesting and productive times in our lives come after we have children. For the majority of us, the greatest challenges and struggles also come in midlife and later. Wholehearted parenting is not having it all figured out and passing it down—it's learning and exploring together. And trust me, there are times when my children are way ahead of me on the journey, either waiting for me or reaching back to pull me along.

As I mentioned in the introduction, if you roughly divide the men and women I've interviewed into two groups—those who feel a deep sense of love and belonging, and those who struggle for it—only one variable separates the groups: Those who feel lovable, who love, and who experience belonging simply believe they are *worthy* of love and belonging. I often say that Wholeheartedness is like the North Star: We never really arrive, but we certainly know if we're headed in the right direction. Raising children who believe in their worthiness requires us to model that journey and that struggle.

The important thing to know about worthiness is that it doesn't have prerequisites. Most of us, on the other hand, have a long list of worthiness prerequisites—qualifiers that we've inherited, learned, and unknowingly picked up along the way. Most of these prerequisites fall in the categories of accomplishments, acquisitions, and external acceptance. It's the *if/when* problem ("I'll be worthy when . . ." or "I'll be worthy if . . ."). They may not be written down, and we may not even be aware of the prerequisites, but we all have a list that says, "I'll be worthy . . ."

- When I lose this weight

- If I get accepted into this school

- If my wife's not cheating

- If we don't get divorced

- If I get promoted

- When I get pregnant

- When he asks me out

- When we buy a house in this neighborhood

- If no one finds out

Shame loves prerequisites. Our if/when worthiness list easily doubles as the gremlins' to-do list. *Don't let her forget that her mom thinks she should lose that baby weight. Remind him that his new boss only respects guys with MBAs. Poke her if she forgets that all of her friends made partner last year.*

As parents, we help our children develop shame resilience and worthiness by staying very mindful about the prerequisites that we're knowingly or unknowingly handing down to them. Are we sending them overt or covert messages about what makes them more and less lovable? Or are we focusing on behaviors that need to change and making it clear that their essential worthiness is not on the table? I often tell parents that some of the most destructive covert messages that we send our children stem from the feminine and masculine norms that we discussed in Chapter 3. Are we overtly or covertly telling our daughters that thin, nice, and modest are prerequisites for worthiness? Are we teaching our girls to respect boys as tender and loving beings? Are we sending messages to our sons that we expect them to be emotionally stoic, to put money and status first, and to be aggressive? Are we teaching our sons to respect women and girls as smart and capable people, not objects?

Perfectionism is another fount of prerequisites. In a dozen years of studying worthiness, I'm convinced that perfectionism is actually contagious. If we struggle with being, living, and looking absolutely perfect, we might as well line our children up and slip those little perfection straitjackets right over their heads. Just as a reminder from Chapter 4, perfectionism is not teaching them how to strive for excellence or be their best selves. Perfectionism is teaching them to value what other people think over what they think or how they feel. It's teaching them to perform, please, and prove. Unfortunately, I have many examples from my own life.

For instance, when Ellen got her first tardy at school, she immediately broke down crying. She was so upset about breaking the rules and upsetting her teacher or the principal that she just fell apart. We kept telling her that it wasn't a big deal and that everyone is late sometimes until she felt better. That evening we celebrated surviving our first tardy with a little "tardy party" after dinner. She finally agreed that it wasn't a big deal and that other people probably didn't judge her for being human.

Fast-forward four days to Sunday morning. We're running late for church and I'm in tears. "Why can't we ever get out of here on time! We're going to be late!" Ellen looked up at me and earnestly asked, "Dad and Charlie will be here in one minute. Are we missing something important?" Without hesitating, I said, "No! I just hate walking in late and sneaking down the aisle. It's the 9 o'clock service, not the 9:05 service." She looked confused for a second, then grinned as she said, "It's not a big deal. Everyone's late sometimes. Remember? I'll throw a tardy party for you when we get home."

Sometimes prerequisites and perfectionism are handed down in very subtle ways. One of the very best pieces of parenting advice that I ever received was from the writer Toni Morrison. It was May of 2000 and Ellen was just shy of her first birthday. Ms. Morrison was on *Oprah* talking about her book *The Bluest Eye*. Oprah said, "Toni says a beautiful thing about the messages that we get about who we are when a child first walks into a room," and she asked Ms. Morrison to talk about it.

Ms. Morrison explained that it's interesting to watch what happens when a child walks into a room. She asked, "Does your face light up?" She explained, "When my children used to walk in the room when they were little, I looked at them to see if they had buckled their trousers or if their hair was combed or if their socks were up. . . . You think your affection and your deep love is on display because you're caring for them. It's not. When they see you, they see the critical face. *What's wrong now?*" Her advice was simple, but paradigm-shifting for me. She said, "Let your face speak what's in your heart. When they walk in the room my face says I'm glad to see them. It's just as small as that, you see?"

I literally think about that advice every day—it's become

a practice. When Ellen comes bounding down the stairs dressed for school, I don't want my first comment to be "Pull your hair back" or "Those shoes don't match your dress." I want my face to convey how happy I am to see her—to be with her. When Charlie comes in the back door and he's sweaty and dirty from catching lizards, I want to flash a smile before I say, "Don't touch anything until you wash your hands." So often we think that we earn parenting points by being critical, put out, and exasperated. Those first looks can be prerequisites or worthiness-builders. I don't want to criticize when my kids walk in the room, I want to light up!

In addition to keeping a mindful eye on prerequisites and perfectionism, we can help our children keep and cultivate their sense of worthiness in another way, one that relates back to what we learned about the differences between shame and guilt. Research indicates that parenting is a primary predictor of how prone our children will be to shame or guilt. In other words, we have a lot of influence over how our kids think about themselves and their struggles. Knowing as we do that shame is positively correlated with addiction, depression, aggression, violence, eating disorders, and suicide, and that guilt is inversely correlated with these outcomes, we naturally would want to raise children who use more guilt self-talk than shame.

This means we need to separate our children from their behaviors. As it turns out, there's a significant difference between *you are bad* and *you did something bad*. And, no, it's not just semantics. Shame corrodes the part of us that believes we can do and be better. When we shame and label our children, we take away their opportunity to grow and try on new behaviors. If a child *tells a lie*, she can change that behavior. If she *is a liar*—where's the potential for change in that?

Cultivating more guilt self-talk and less shame self-talk

requires rethinking how we discipline and talk to our children. But it also means explaining these concepts to our kids. Children are very receptive to talking about shame if we're willing to do it. By the time they're four and five, we can explain to them the difference between guilt and shame, and how much we love them even when they make bad choices.

When Ellen was in kindergarten, her teacher called me at home one afternoon and said, "I totally get what you do now."

When I asked her why, she said that earlier in the week, she had looked over at Ellen, who was in the "Glitter Center" and said, "Ellen! You're a mess." Apparently, Ellen got a very serious look on her face and said, "I may be making a mess, but I'm not a mess." (That's the day I became "that parent.")

Charlie also gets the distinction between shame and guilt. When I found our dog pulling food out of the trash can, I scolded her by saying, "Bad girl!" Charlie came sliding around the corner, shouting, "Daisy is a good girl who made a bad choice! We love her! We just don't love her choices!"

When I tried to explain the difference by saying, "Daisy is a dog, Charlie," his response was, "Oh, I see. Daisy is a good dog who made a bad choice."

Shame is so painful for children because it is inextricably linked to the fear of being unlovable. For young children who are still dependent on their parents for survival—for food, shelter, and safety—feeling unlovable is a threat to survival. It's trauma. I'm convinced that the reason most of us revert back to feeling childlike and small when we're in shame is because our brain stores our early shame experiences as trauma, and when it's triggered we return to that place. We don't have the neurobiological research yet to confirm this, but I've coded hundreds of interviews that follow this same pattern:

"I don't know what happened. My boss called me an idiot in front of my team and I couldn't respond. All of a sudden I'm back in Mrs. Porter's second-grade class and I'm speechless. I can't come back with one decent response."

Or

"My son struck out for the second time and I couldn't see straight. I always said I'd never do what my dad did to me, but there I was screaming at him in front of his teammates. I'm not even sure how it happened."

In Chapter 3 we learned that the brain processes social rejection or shame the same exact way it processes physical pain. I suspect we'll eventually have the data to support my hypothesis about children storing shame as trauma, but in the meantime I can say without hesitation that **childhood experiences of shame change who we are, how we think about ourselves, and our sense of self-worth.**

We can work hard not to use shame as a parenting tool, but our children are still going to encounter shame in the outside world. The good news is that when children understand the distinction between shame and guilt, and when they know that we're interested and open to talking about these feelings and experiences, they are much more likely to talk to us about the shaming experiences they may encounter with teachers, coaches, clergy, babysitters, grandparents, and other adults who have influence in their lives. This is critically important because it gives us the opportunity to "crop" shame the way we do photographs.

I often use a scrapbook as a metaphor to talk about the impact shame has on children. As parents, once we learn about shame, we will more than likely realize that, yes, we've shamed our children. It happens. Even to shame researchers. Given the severity of the outcomes around shame, we'll also begin to worry that the shaming moments that happen outside our home will define our children, despite our best efforts in the family. And those experiences will happen—name calling, put-downs, and teasing are rampant in our culture of cruelty. The good news, however, is that we have a lot of influence over how much power those experiences have in our children's lives.

Most of us can remember shaming events from childhood that felt defining. But more than likely we remember them because we didn't process those experiences with parents who were open to talking about shame and committed to helping us cultivate shame resilience. I don't blame my parents for that any more than I judge my grandmother letting me stand next to her in the front seat while she was driving. They didn't have access to the information we have today.

Knowing what I do now, I think about shame and worthiness in this way: "It's the album, not the picture." If you imagine opening up a photo album, and many of the pages are full of eight-by-ten photos of shaming events, you'll close that album and walk away thinking, *Shame defines that story.* If, on the other hand, you open that album and see a few small photos of shame experiences, but each one is surrounded by pictures of worthiness, hope, struggle, resilience, courage, failure, success, and vulnerability, the shame experiences are only a part of a larger story. They don't define the album.

Again, we can't shameproof our children. Our task instead is teaching and modeling shame resilience, and that starts with conversations about what shame is and how it shows up in our lives. The adults I interviewed who were raised by parents who used shame as a primary parenting tool had much more difficulty believing in their worthiness than the participants who experienced shame occasionally and were able to talk about it with their parents.

If you have grown children and are wondering if it's too late to teach shame resilience or to change the album, the answer is no. It's not too late. The power of owning our stories, even the difficult ones, is that we get to write the ending. Several years ago, I received a letter from a woman who wrote:

> Your work changed my life in a very strange way. My mom saw you speak at a church in Amarillo. Afterwards, she wrote me a long letter that said, "I had no idea there was a difference between shame and guilt. I think I shamed you your entire life. I meant to use guilt. I never thought you weren't good enough. I did not like your choices. But I shamed you. I can't take that back, but I need you to know that you're the best thing that ever happened to me and I'm so proud to be your mother." I couldn't believe it. My mom is seventy-five and I'm fifty-five. It healed so much. And it changed everything, including the way I parent my own kids.

In addition to helping our children understand shame, and use guilt self-talk rather than shame self-talk, we have to be very careful about shame leakage. Even if we don't shame our children, shame still shows up in our lives in ways that can have a powerful affect on our family. Basically, we can't raise children who are more shame resilient than we are. I can encourage Ellen to love her body, but what really matters are the observations she makes about my relationship with my own body. *Damn it.* I can soothe Charlie's concerns that he might run the wrong direction around the bases by telling him that he doesn't have to fully understand the ins and outs of baseball before his first T-ball game, but does he observe me and Steve trying new things, making mistakes, and failing without becoming self-critical? Damn it. Again.

Lastly, normalizing is one of the most powerful shame-resilience tools that we can offer our children. Like I explained in the last chapter, normalizing means helping our children know they're not alone and that we've experienced many of the same struggles. This applies to social situations, changes in their bodies, shaming experiences, feeling left out, and wanting to be brave but feeling afraid. There's something sacred that happens between a parent and a child when the parent says, "Me too!" or shares a personal story that relates to their child's struggle.

MINDING THE GAP: SUPPORTING OUR CHILDREN MEANS SUPPORTING EACH OTHER

I believe it's important at this point to pause to recognize the shaming nature of parenting "values" debates. When you listen to conversations, or read books and blogs, about controversial and/or divisive issues in parenting, like how and where women labor, circumcision, vaccinations, co-sleeping, feeding, etc., what you hear is shame and what you see is hurt. Deep hurt. You see people—mostly mothers—engaging in the exact same behaviors that I earlier defined as shaming: name calling, put-downs, and bullying.

Here's what I've come to believe about these behaviors: **You can't claim to care about the welfare of children if you're shaming other parents for the choices they're**

making. Those are mutually exclusive behaviors and they create a huge values gap. Yes, most of us (myself included) have strong opinions on every one of those topics, but if we really care about the broader welfare of children, our job is to make choices that are aligned with our values and support other parents who are doing the same. Our job is also to tend to our own worthiness. When we feel good about the choices we're making and when we're engaging with the world from a place of worthiness rather than scarcity, we feel no need to judge and attack.

It's easy to put up a straw man in this argument and say, "So we're just supposed to ignore parents who are abusing their children?" Fact: That someone is making different choices from us doesn't in itself constitute abuse. If there's real abuse happening, by all means, call the police. If not, we shouldn't call it abuse. As a social worker who spent a year interning at Child Protective Services, I have little tolerance for debates that casually use the terms *abuse* or *neglect* to scare or belittle parents who are simply doing things that we judge as wrong, different, or bad.

In fact, I've sworn off the good-bad parenting dichotomy simply because on any given day you could file me under both good parent and bad parent, depending on your perspective and how things are going for me. I just don't see what value this judgmental frame adds to our lives or to the larger parenting conversation. In fact, it's a shame storm waiting to happen. To me the question of parenting values is about engagement. Are we paying attention? Thinking through our choices? Open to learning and being wrong? Curious and willing to ask questions?

What I've learned from my work is that there are a million ways out in the world to be a wonderful, engaged parent, and some of them are going to bump up against what I personally think about parenting. For example, Steve and I are very strict about what we let the kids watch on TV—especially when it comes to violence. We think about it, talk about it, and make the best decisions we can. On the other hand, we've got friends who let their children watch movies and shows that we don't allow Ellen or Charlie watch. But you know what? They also think about it, talk about it, and make the best decisions they can. They just came to a different conclusion than we did, and I respect that.

We recently found ourselves on the other side of this issue when some good friends expressed surprise that we let Ellen read *The Hunger Games*. Again, those parents were also engaged in the question, and the conversation we had showed mutual respect and empathy. Minding the gap can be particularly challenging when honoring difference is one of our aspirational values. I think the key is remembering that when other parents make different choices than we're making, it's not necessarily criticism. Daring greatly means finding our own path and respecting what that search looks like for other folks.

MINDING THE GAP AND BELONGING

Worthiness is about love *and* belonging, and one of the best ways to show our children that our love for them is unconditional is to make sure they know they belong in our families. I know that sounds strange, but it's a very powerful and at times heart-wrenching issue for children. On page 145, I defined *belonging* as the innate human desire to be part of something larger than us. One of the biggest surprises in this research was learning that fitting in and belonging are not the same thing. In fact, fitting in is one of the greatest barriers to belonging. Fitting in is about assessing a situation and becoming who you need to be in order to be accepted. Belonging, on the other hand, doesn't require us to *change* who we are; it requires us to *be* who we are.

When I asked a large group of eighth graders to break into small teams and come up with the differences between *fitting in* and *belonging*, their answers floored me:

- *Belonging* is being somewhere where you want to be, and they want you. *Fitting in* is being somewhere where you really want to be, but they don't care one way or the other.

- *Belonging* is being accepted for you. *Fitting in* is being accepted for being like everyone else.

- I get to be me if I belong. I have to be like you to fit in.

They nailed the definitions. It doesn't matter where in the country I ask this question, or what type of school I'm visiting, middle and high school students understand how this works.

They also talk openly about the heartache of not feeling a sense of belonging at home. That first time I asked the eighth graders to come up with the definitions, one student wrote, "Not belonging at school is really hard. But it's nothing compared to what it feels like when you don't belong at home." When I asked the students what that meant, they used these examples:

- Not living up to your parents' expectations

- Not being as cool or popular as your parents want you to be

- Not being as smart as your parents

- Not being good at the same things your parents were good at

- Your parents being embarrassed because you don't have enough friends or you're not an athlete or a cheerleader

- Your parents not liking who you are and what you like to do

- When your parents don't pay attention to your life

If we want to cultivate worthiness in our children, we need to make sure they know that they belong and that their belonging is unconditional. What makes that such a challenge is that most of us struggle to feel a sense of belonging—to know that we're a part of something, not *despite* our vulnerabilities, but *because* of them. We can't give our children what we don't have, which means we have to work to cultivate a sense of belonging alongside our children. Here's an example of how we can grow together and how our children are capable of great empathy. (There's nothing that inspires that deep sense of belonging like shared empathy!)

When Ellen was in fourth grade, she came home from school one day and burst into tears as soon as we shut the front door, then ran up to her room. I immediately followed, then knelt down in front of her and asked her what was wrong. Through her sniffles she said, "I'm so tired of being *the other*! I'm sick of it!"

I didn't understand, so I asked her to explain what she meant by "the other."

"We play soccer every day at recess. Two popular kids are the captains and they pick the teams. The first captain says, 'I'll take Suzie, John, Pete, Robin, and Jake.' The second captain says, 'I'll take Andrew, Steve, Katie, and Sue, and we can split *the others*.' Every single day I'm one of *the others*. I never get to be named."

My heart sank. She was sitting on the edge of her bed with her head in her hands. I was so concerned when I followed her into her room that I hadn't even flipped on the light. I couldn't stand the vulnerability of seeing her sitting in the dark crying, so I walked over to the light switch. It was divine intervention—the act of starting to turn on the lights to alleviate my discomfort made me think of my favorite quote about darkness and compassion from Pema Chödrön, who writes: "Compassion is not a relationship between the healer and the wounded. It's a relationship between equals. Only when we know our own darkness well can we be present with the darkness of others. Compassion becomes real when we recognize our shared humanity."

I left the light switch alone and walked back to sit with Ellen in the literal and emotional dark. I put my arm around her shoulder and said, "I know what it's like to be the other."

She wiped her nose on the back of her hand and said, "No, you don't. You're really popular."

I explained that I really do know what it feels like. I told her, "When I feel like the other, I get angry and hurt, and I mostly feel small and lonely. I don't need to be popular, but I want people to recognize me and treat me like I matter. Like I belong."

She couldn't believe it. "You do know! That's exactly how I feel!"

We snuggled on her bed, and she told me about her recess

experiences, and I told her about some of my experiences in school when otherness is both powerful and painful.

About two weeks later, we were both at home when the mail arrived. I ran to the door with great anticipation. I was scheduled to speak at a star-studded event, and I was dying to see the publicity poster. It seems weird now, but I was so excited at the idea of seeing my photo next to the pictures of the movie stars. I sat down on the couch with the poster, I unrolled it, and I started scanning like a madwoman. Just as I was doing this, Ellen walked in and said, "Cool! Is that your poster? Let me see!"

As she walked over to the couch, she could tell my mood had changed from anticipation to disappointment. "What's wrong, Mom?"

I patted the couch and she sat down next to me. I held the poster open, and she traced the pictures with her finger. "I don't see you. Where are you?"

I pointed to a line on the poster under the celebrity photos that said, "And others."

Ellen leaned back against the sofa cushions, put her head on my shoulder, and said, "Oh, Mom, I think you're the others. I'm sorry."

I didn't reply right away. I was feeling small both because there was no picture and for caring that there was no picture. Ellen leaned forward, looked at me, and said, "I know what that feels like. When I'm the other, I feel hurt and small and lonely. We all want to matter and belong."

It turned out to be one of the best moments of my life. We may not always have a sense of belonging on the recess playground or at a big, fancy conference, but in that moment we knew that we belonged where it mattered the most—at home. Parenting perfection is not the goal. In fact, the best gifts—

the best teaching moments—happen in those imperfect moments when we allow children to help us mind the gap.

Here's a powerful story about cultivating shame resilience and minding the gap from Susan, a woman I interviewed a couple of years ago. Susan was busy talking to a group of mothers at her kids' school while her kids were standing close by waiting for her to take them home. The mothers were discussing who would host the "Welcome Kinder Kids" party for the new students. They all hated the thought of doing it, but the one woman who volunteered to throw the party had "a filthy house." After talking about this woman and her house for a few minutes, they agreed that letting her host the party would reflect poorly on them and the PTO.

When they finished their discussion, Susan loaded up the kids (a daughter in kinder, and two sons—one in first grade and another in third grade) and started home. Susan's first-grade son randomly called out from the backseat, "I think you're a great mom." Susan smiled and said, "Well, thank you." A few minutes after they walked in the house, the same child came up to her with big tears in his eyes. He looked at Susan and said, "Do you feel bad about yourself? Are you okay?"

Susan said she was completely taken by surprise. She knelt down and said, "No. Why? What's wrong?"

Her son replied, "You always say that when people get together and talk bad about someone just because they are different, it means they might feel bad about themselves. You said that when we feel good about who we are, we don't say mean things about other people."

Susan immediately recognized the warm wash of shame. She knew that her son had overheard the conversation at the school.

This is the moment. The Wholehearted parenting moment. Can we tolerate the vulnerability long enough to be with it for a minute? Or do we need to discharge the shame and discomfort by redirecting our child or blaming them for "crossing a line?" Can we take this opportunity to acknowledge how wonderfully he's practicing empathy? Can we make mistakes and make amends? If we want our kids to own and be honest about their experiences, can we own ours?

Susan looked at her son and said, "Thank you so much for checking on me and asking me how I feel. I feel okay, but I think I made a mistake. I need a little time to think about all of this. You're right about one thing—I was saying hurtful things."

After Susan pulled herself together, she sat down with her son and they talked. They discussed how easy it is to get caught up in a group situation where everyone is talking about someone. Susan was honest and admitted that she sometimes struggles with "what people think." She said her son leaned into her and whispered, "Me too." They promised to keep talking to each other about their experiences.

Engagement means investing time and energy. It means sitting down with our children and understanding their worlds, their interests, and their stories. Engaged parents can be found on both sides of all of the controversial parenting debates. They come from different values, traditions, and cultures. What they share in common is practicing the values. What they seem to share is a philosophy of "I'm not perfect and I'm not always right, but I'm here, open, paying attention, loving you, and fully engaged."

There is no question that engagement requires sacrifice, but that's what we signed up for when we decided to become parents. Most of us have so many competing demands on our time that it's easy to think, *I can't sacrifice three hours to sit down and review my son's Facebook page or sit with my daughter while she explains every detail of the fourth grade science fair scandal.* I struggle with that too. But Jimmy Grace, a priest from our Episcopal church, recently gave a sermon about the nature of sacrifice and it totally shifted how I think about parenting. He explained that in its original Latin form, *sacrifice* means *to make sacred* or *to make holy.* I Wholeheartedly believe that when we are fully engaged in parenting, regardless of how imperfect, vulnerable, and messy it is, we are creating something sacred.

THE COURAGE TO BE VULNERABLE

Before writing this section, I spread my data all over my dining room table and asked myself this question: What do parents experience as the most vulnerable and bravest thing that they do in their efforts to raise Wholehearted children? I thought it would take days to figure it out, but as I looked over the field notes, the answer was obvious: letting their children struggle and experience adversity.

As I travel across the country there seems to be growing concern on the part of parents and teachers that children are not learning how to handle adversity or disappointment because we're always rescuing and protecting them. What's interesting is that more often than not, I hear this concern from the same parents who are chronically intervening, rescuing, and protecting. It's not that our children can't stand the vulnerability of handling their own situations, it's that we can't stand the uncertainty, risk, and emotional exposure, even when we know it's the right thing to do.

I used to struggle with letting go and allowing my children to find their own way, but something that I learned in the research dramatically changed my perspective and I no longer see rescuing and intervening as unhelpful, I now think about it as dangerous. Don't get me wrong—I still struggle and I still step in when I shouldn't, but I now think twice before I let my discomfort dictate my behaviors. Here's why: **Hope is a function of struggle.** If we want our children to develop high levels of hopefulness, we have to let them struggle. And let me tell you, next to love and belonging, I'm not sure I want anything more for my kids than a deep sense of hopefulness.

Experience with adversity, tenacity, and grit emerged in my research as an important quality of Wholeheartedness. I was so grateful to see it because it was one of the few qualities of Wholeheartedness that I had at the time (remember in the introduction—I was two for ten). When I went into the literature to search for a concept that had all of these elements, I found C. R. Snyder's research on hope. I was shocked. First, I thought hope was a warm, fuzzy emotion—the feeling of possibility. Second, I was looking for something that I had thought of as *being scrappy* and nicknamed "Plan B"—these folks could turn to *Plan B* when Plan A fell apart.

As it turns out, I was wrong about hope and right about scrappy and *Plan B*. According to Snyder, who dedicated his career to studying this topic, hope isn't an emotion; it's a way of thinking or a cognitive process. Emotions play a supporting role, but hope is really a thought process made up of what Snyder calls a trilogy of goals, pathways, and agency. In very simple terms, hope happens when:

- We have the ability to set realistic goals (*I know where I want to go*).

- We are able to figure out how to achieve those goals, including the ability to stay flexible and develop alternative routes (*I know how to get there, I'm persistent, and I can tolerate disappointment and try again*).

- We believe in ourselves (*I can do this!*).

So, hope is a combination of setting goals, having the tenacity and perseverance to pursue them, and believing in our own abilities. Hope is *Plan B*.

And, here's the part that inspired me to deal with my own vulnerability so I could step back and let my children learn how to figure some things out on their own: Hope is learned! According to Snyder, children most often learn hope from their parents. To learn hopefulness, children need relationships that are characterized by boundaries, consistency, and support. Children with high levels of hopefulness have experience with adversity. They've been given the opportunity to struggle and in doing that they learn how to believe in themselves.

Raising children who are hopeful and who have the courage to be vulnerable means stepping back and letting them experience disappointment, deal with conflict, learn how to assert themselves, and have the opportunity to fail. **If we're always following our children into the arena, hushing the critics, and assuring their victory, they'll never learn that they have the ability to dare greatly on their own.**

One of my best lessons on this comes from an experience that I had with Ellen. It began when I was still ten cars away from her in the swim team pickup line. It was getting dark, so I could only make out her silhouette, but that was enough: I could tell something was wrong by the way she was standing. She flung herself into the front seat, and before I could ask her about practice, she was in tears.

"What happened? What's wrong? Are you okay?"

She stared out the window, drew a deep breath as she wiped her tears on the sleeve of her hoodie, and said, "I have to swim the 100 breaststroke at the meet on Saturday."

I knew this was a really bad thing in her world, so I tried not to seem relieved—which I was because, in a crazy-but-normal-for-me fashion, I was already thinking something really horrible had happened.

"You don't understand. I can't swim breaststroke. I'm terrible. You don't get it. I begged him not to put me in that event."

I was getting ready to respond with something empathetic and encouraging as I pulled into the driveway, but just then she looked me right in the eyes, put her hand on top of my hand, and said, "Please, Mom. Please help me. I'm still going to be swimming when the other girls are getting out of the pool and the next heat is getting on the blocks. I'm really that slow."

I couldn't swallow. I couldn't think clearly. All of a sudden, I'm ten years old and I'm on the blocks getting ready to swim for the Memorial Northwest Marlins. My dad is the starter, and he's giving me the win-or-die look. I'm in the lane closest to the wall—the slow lane. It's going to be a disaster. Moments earlier, as I was sitting on the ready bench contemplating making a run for my banana-seat bike leaning against the fence by the diving boards, I overheard the coach say, "Let's just swim her up an age group. I'm not sure she can finish the race, but it will be interesting."

"Mom? Mom?? Mom!!! Are you listening to me? Will

you help me? Will you talk to the coach and see if he'll put me in another race?"

The vulnerability felt unbearable and I wanted to scream, "Yes! You don't have to swim any event that you don't want to swim. EVER!" But I didn't. Calm was one of my new Wholehearted practices, so I took a deep breath, counted to five, and said, "Let me talk to your dad."

After the kids went to bed, Steve and I spent an hour debating the issue and finally agreed that she would have to take it up with her coach. If he wanted her to swim that race, she needed to swim it. As right as the decision felt, I hated every minute of it, and I tried everything from picking a fight with Steve to blaming the coach to venting my fear and discharging the vulnerability.

Ellen was upset when we told her this, and even more upset when she came home from practice and told us that her coach thought it was important for her to get an official time for the event. She folded her arms on the table, put her head down, and cried. At one point she lifted up her head and said, "I could just scratch the event. A lot of people miss their heats." A part of me thought, *Perfect!* But then she said, "I won't win. I'm not even good enough to get second or third place. Everyone is going to be watching."

This was the opportunity to move the levers—to redefine what's important to her. To make our family culture more influential than the swim meet, her friends, and the ultracompetitive sports culture that is rampant in our community. I looked at her and said, "You can scratch that event. I'd probably consider that option too. But what if your goal for that race isn't to win or even to get out of the water at the same time as the other girls? What if your goal is to show up and get wet?"

She looked at me as if I was crazy. "Just show up and get in the water?"

I explained that I had spent many years never trying anything that I wasn't already good at doing, and how those choices almost made me forget what it feels like to be brave. I said, "Sometimes the bravest and most important thing you can do is just show up."

Steve and I made sure that we weren't with her when her heat was called. When it was time for the girls to get on the blocks, I wasn't sure if she'd be there, but she was. We stood at the end of her lane and held our breath. She looked right at us, nodded her head, and snapped her goggles into place.

She was the last one out of the pool. The other swimmers had already left the deck, and there were girls standing on the blocks ready for the next heat. Steve and I screamed and cheered the entire time. When she got out of the pool, she walked over to her coach, who gave her a hug, then showed her something about her kick. When she finally made her way to us, she was smiling and a little tearful. She looked at her dad and me and said, "That was pretty bad, but I did it. I showed up and I got wet. I was brave."

I wrote the following parenting manifesto because I need it. Steve and I need it. Putting down the measuring stick in a culture that uses acquisitions and accomplishments to assess worth is not easy. I use the manifesto as a touchstone, a prayer, and a meditation when I'm wrestling with vulnerability or when I've got that "never enough" fear. It reminds me of the finding that changed and probably saved my life: *Who we are and how we engage with the world are much stronger predictors of how our children will do than what we know about parenting.*

The Wholehearted Parenting Manifesto

Above all else, I want you to know that you are loved and lovable.

You will learn this from my words and actions—the lessons on love are in how I treat you and how I treat myself.

I want you to engage with the world from a place of worthiness.

You will learn that you are worthy of love, belonging, and joy every time you see me practice self-compassion and embrace my own imperfections.

We will practice courage in our family by showing up, letting ourselves be seen, and honoring vulnerability. We will share our stories of struggle and strength. There will always be room in our home for both.

We will teach you compassion by practicing compassion with ourselves first; then with each other. We will set and respect boundaries; we will honor hard work, hope, and perseverance. Rest and play will be family values, as well as family practices.

You will learn accountability and respect by watching me make mistakes and make amends, and by watching how I ask for what I need and talk about how I feel.

I want you to know joy, so together we will practice gratitude.

I want you to *feel* joy, so together we will learn how to be vulnerable.

When uncertainty and scarcity visit, you will be able to draw from the spirit that is a part of our everyday life.

Together we will cry and face fear and grief. I will

want to take away your pain, but instead I will sit with you and teach you how to feel it.

We will laugh and sing and dance and create. We will always have permission to be ourselves with each other. No matter what, you will always belong here.

As you begin your Wholehearted journey, the greatest gift that I can give to you is to live and love with my whole heart and to dare greatly.

I will not teach or love or show you anything perfectly, but I will let you see me, and I will always hold sacred the gift of seeing you. Truly, deeply, seeing you.

You can download a copy of this manifesto from my website (www.brene brown.com).

FINAL THOUGHTS

It is not the critic who counts; not the man who points out how the strong man stumbles, or where the doer of deeds could have done them better.

The credit belongs to the man who is actually in the arena, whose face is marred by dust and sweat and blood; who strives valiantly; who errs, who comes short again and again,

because there is no effort without error and short-coming; but who does actually strive to do the deeds; who knows great enthusiasms, the great devotions; who spends himself in a worthy cause;

who at the best knows in the end the triumph of high achievement, and who at the worst, if he fails, at least fails while daring greatly. . . .
　　　　　　　　　　　　　—Theodore Roosevelt

In the nine months that it took me to shape and prune a dozen years of research into this book, I've revisited this quote at least one hundred times. And truthfully, I normally come back to it in fits of rage or with tearstained desperation, thinking, *Maybe this is all bullshit*, or *It's not worth the vulnerability*. Just recently, after enduring a few really mean-spirited anonymous comments from a news website, I pulled the quote down from the pinboard over my desk and spoke directly to the sheet of paper, "If the critic doesn't count, then why does this hurt so much?"

The paper didn't respond.

As I held the quote in my hand, I remembered a conversation that I had just had with a guy in his very early twenties. He told me that his parents sent him links to my TED talks and he really liked the idea of Wholeheartedness and daring greatly. When he told me that the talks inspired him to tell the young woman he's been dating for several months that he loved her, I winced and hoped for a happy ending to the story.

No such luck. She told him that she thought he was "awesome" but that she thought they should date other people. When he got back to his apartment after talking to his girlfriend, he told his two roommates what had happened. He said, "They were both hunched over their laptops and without looking up one of them was like 'What were you thinking, man?'" One of his roommates told him that girls only like guys who are running the other way. He looked at me and said, "I felt pretty stupid at first. For a second I was mad at myself and even a little pissed at you. But then I thought about it and I remembered why I did it. I told my roommates, 'I was daring greatly, dude.'"

He smiled when he told me, "They stopped typing, looked at me, nodded their heads, and said, 'Oh. Right on, dude.'"

Daring greatly is not about winning or losing. It's about courage. In a world where scarcity and shame dominate and feeling afraid has become second nature, vulnerability is subversive. Uncomfortable. It's even a little dangerous at times. And, without question, putting ourselves out there means there's a far greater risk of feeling hurt. But as I look back on my own life and what Daring Greatly has meant to me, I can honestly say that nothing is as uncomfortable, dangerous, and hurtful as believing that I'm standing on the outside of my life looking in and wondering what it would be like if I had the courage to show up and let myself be seen.

So, Mr. Roosevelt . . . I think you nailed it. There really is "no effort without error and shortcoming" and there really is no triumph without vulnerability. Now when I read that quote, even when I'm feeling kicked around, all I can think is, *Right on, dude.*

APPENDIX

Trust in Emergence:
Grounded Theory and My Research Process

Caminante, no hay camino, se hace camino al andar.

Traveler, there is no path, the path must be forged as you walk.

This line from the Spanish poet Antonio Machado captures the spirit of my research process and the theories that emerged from that process. Initially I set out, on what I thought was a well-traveled path, to find empirical evidence of what I knew to be true. I soon realized that conducting research centering on what matters to research participants—grounded theory research—means there is no path and, certainly, there is no way of knowing what you will find.

The most difficult challenges of becoming a grounded theory researcher are:

1. Acknowledging that it is virtually impossible to understand grounded theory methodology prior to using it,
2. Developing the courage to let the research participants define the research problem, and
3. Letting go of your own interests and preconceived ideas to "trust in emergence."

Ironically (or maybe not), these are also the challenges of Daring Greatly and living a courageous life.

Below is an overview of the design, methodology, sampling, and coding processes that I use in my research. Before we jump in, I want to acknowledge Barney Glaser and Anselm Strauss for their pioneering work in qualitative research and for developing grounded theory methodology. And, to Dr. Glaser, who was willing to commute from California to serve as the methodologist on my dissertation committee at the University of Houston: You literally changed the way I see the world.

THE RESEARCH JOURNEY

As a doctoral student, the power of statistics and the clean lines of quantitative research appealed to me, but I fell in love with the richness and depth of qualitative research. Storytelling is my DNA, and I couldn't resist the idea of research as story-catching. Stories are data with a soul and no methodology honors that more than grounded theory. The mandate of grounded theory is to develop theories based on people's lived experiences rather than proving or disproving existing theories.

Behavioral researcher Fred Kerlinger defines theory as "a set of interrelated constructs or concepts, definitions, and propositions that present a systematic view of phenomena specifying relations among variables, with the purpose of explaining and predicting the phenomena." In grounded theory we don't start with a problem or a hypothesis or a literature review, we start with a topic. We let the participants define the problem or their main concern about the topic, we develop a theory, and then we see how and where it fits in the literature.

I didn't sign on to study shame—one of the most (if not the most) complex and multifaceted emotions that we experience. A topic that not only took me six years to understand, but an emotion that is so powerful that the mere mention of the word *shame* triggers discomfort and avoidance in people. I innocently started with an interest in learning more about the anatomy of connection.

After fifteen years of social work education, I was sure of one thing: Connection is why we're here; it is what gives purpose and meaning to our lives. The power that connection holds in our lives was confirmed when the main concern about connection emerged as the fear of disconnection; the fear that something we've done or failed to do, something about who we are or where we come from, has made us unlovable and unworthy of connection. I learned that we resolve this concern by understanding our vulnerabilities and cultivating empathy, courage, and compassion—what I call shame resilience.

After developing a theory on shame resilience, and getting clear about the effect of scarcity on our lives, I wanted to dig deeper—I wanted to know more. The problem is that there's only so much you can understand about shame and scarcity by asking about shame and scarcity. I needed another approach to get under the experiences. That's when I had the idea to borrow a few principles from chemistry.

In chemistry, especially thermodynamics, if you have an element or property that is too volatile to measure, you often have to rely on indirect measurement. You measure the property by combining and reducing related, less volatile compounds until those relationships and manipulations reveal a measurement of your original property. My idea was to learn more about shame and scarcity by exploring what exists in their absence.

I know how people experience and move through shame, but what are people feeling, doing, and thinking when shame doesn't constantly have a knife to their throats, threatening them with being unworthy of connection? How are some people living right alongside us in this culture of scarcity and still holding on to the belief that they are enough? I knew these people existed because I had interviewed them and used some of the incidents from their data to inform my work on empathy and shame resilience.

Before I dove back into the data, I named this study "Wholehearted Living." I was looking for women and men living and loving with their whole hearts despite the risks and uncertainty. I wanted to know what they had in common. What were their main concerns, and what were the patterns and themes that defined their Wholeheartedness? I reported the findings from that study in *The Gifts of Imperfection* and an academic journal article that will be published in late 2012 or early 2013.

Vulnerability has consistently emerged as a core category in my work. It was a critical component in both my study on shame and my study on Wholeheartedness, and there's even a chapter on it in my dissertation on connection. I understood the relationships between vulnerability and the other emotions that I've studied, but after years of dropping deeper and deeper into this work, I wanted to know more about vulnerability and how it worked. The grounded theory that emerged from this investigation is the subject of this book and another academic article in press.

DESIGN

As I've mentioned, grounded theory methodology, as originally developed by Glaser and Strauss and refined by Glaser informed the plan of research for my studies. The grounded theory process consists of five basic components: theoretical sensitivity, theoretical sampling, coding, theoretical memoing, and sorting. These five components were integrated by the constant-comparison method of data analysis. The goal of the research was to understand the participants' "main concerns" related to experiencing the topic being examined (e.g., shame, Wholeheartedness, vulnerability). Once the main concerns emerged from the data, I developed a theory that explains how the participants continually resolve their concerns in their daily lives.

SAMPLE

Theoretical sampling, the process of data collection that allows for the generation of theory, was the primary sampling method that I used in this study. When using theoretical sampling, the researcher simultaneously collects, codes, and analyzes data and uses this ongoing process to determine what data to collect next and where to find them. In line with theoretical sampling, I selected participants based on the analysis and coding interviews and secondary data.

One important tenet of grounded theory is the idea that researchers should not assume the relevance of identity data, including race, age, gender, sexual orientation, class, and ability. Although the relevance of these variables was not assumed, purposive sampling (intentionally sampling across identity data) was used with theoretical sampling to ensure that a diverse group of participants were interviewed. At certain points during my research, identity data indeed emerged as relevant, and in these cases purposive sampling continued to inform the theoretical sample. In categories where identity did not emerge as relevant, theoretical sampling was used exclusively.

I interviewed 750 female participants, approximately 43 percent of whom identified themselves as Caucasian, 30 percent as African-American, 18 percent as Latina, and 9 percent as Asian-American. The female participants' ages ranged from eighteen to eighty-eight years, with a mean of forty-one. I interviewed 530 men, approximately 40 percent of whom identified themselves as Caucasian, 25 percent as African-American, 20 percent as Latino, and 15 percent identified as Asian. The mean age of the men interviewed was forty-six (the range was eighteen to eighty).

Although grounded-theory methodology often yields theoretical saturation (the point at which no new conceptual insights are generated and the researcher has provided repeated evidence for his or her conceptual categories) with far fewer than my total 1,280 participants, three interrelated theories emerged with multiple core categories and numerous properties informing each category. The nuanced and complex nature of shame resilience, Wholeheartedness, and vulnerability necessitated the large sample size.

A basic tenet of grounded theory is "all is data." Glaser writes, "The briefest comment to the lengthiest interview, written words in magazines, books and newspapers, documents, observations, biases of self and others, spurious variables, or whatever else may come the researcher's way in his substantive area of research is data for grounded theory."

In addition to the 1,280 participant interviews, I analyzed field notes that I had taken on sensitizing literature, conversations with content experts, and field notes from my meetings with graduate students who conducted participant interviews and assisted with the literature analysis. Additionally, I recorded and coded field notes on the experience of taking approximately 400 master and doctoral social-worker students through my graduate course on shame, vulnerability, and empathy, and training an estimated 15,000 mental health and addiction professionals.

I also coded over 3,500 pieces of secondary data. These include clinical case studies and case notes, letters, and journal pages. In total, I coded approximately 11,000 incidents (phrases and sentences from the original field notes) using the constant comparative method (line-by-line analysis). I did all of this coding manually, as software is not recommended in Glaserian-grounded theory.

I collected all of the data with the exception of 215 participant interviews that were conducted by graduate social-work students working under my direction. In order to ensure inter-rater reliability, I trained all research assistants and I coded and analyzed all of their field notes.

Approximately half of the interviews were individual meetings and the other half happened in dyads, triads, and groups. Interview times ranged from forty-five minutes to three hours, with an average of approximately sixty minutes. Adjusted conversational interviewing was utilized because it is regarded as the most effective grounded theory approach to interviewing.

CODING

I used the constant comparative method to analyze the data line by line, and then I developed memos to capture the emergent concepts and their relationships. The primary focus of the analysis was identifying the participants' main concerns and the emergence of a core variable. As I conducted additional interviews, I reconceptualized categories and identified the properties that inform each category. I used selective coding when core concepts emerged and the data were saturated across categories and across their properties.

Grounded theory researchers are required to conceptualize from the data. This approach is very different from traditional qualitative methods that yield findings based on thick description of data and participant quotes. To conceptualize shame, Wholeheartedness, and vulnerability, and to identify the participants' main concerns about these topics, I analyzed data line by line while asking the following questions: What are the participants describing? What do they care about? What are they worried about? What are the participants trying to do? What explains the different behaviors, thoughts, and actions? Again, I used the constant comparative method to reexamine the data against the emerging categories and their related properties.

LITERATURE ANALYSIS

For the same reasons the grounded theorist allows the research problem to emerge from the data, a full review of the significant literature is conducted after the theory is generated from the data. The literature reviews done in quantitative research and traditional qualitative research serve as buttresses on both sides of research findings—literature reviews are conducted to support the need for new research, the research is conducted, findings emerge independent of the literature, and the research is again supported by the literature to demonstrate its contribution to the researcher's profession.

In grounded theory, data buttress the theory and the literature is part of the data. I learned very quickly that grounded-theory researchers cannot go into the literature review thinking, *The theory has emerged, I'm done, how does it fit?* Instead, the grounded theorist must understand that the literature review is actually a literature analysis and it is not separate from the research but is a continuation of the process.

The references and related research quoted in this book both supported and informed the emerging theories.

EVALUATING GROUNDED THEORY

According to Glaser, grounded theories are evaluated by assessing their fit, relevance, workability, and modifiability. The theory has achieved "fit" when the categories of the theory fit the data. Violations of fit occur when data are forced into preformed categories or discarded in favor of keeping an existing theory intact.

In addition to fit, the theory must be relevant to the action of the area. Grounded theories are relevant when they allow the core problems and processes to emerge. Workability is achieved if the theory can explain what happened, predict what will happen, and interpret what is happening in an area of substantive or formal inquiry. There are two criteria for evaluating whether a theory "works"—the categories must fit and the theory must "work the core of what is going on." *Working the core* means that the researcher has conceptualized the data in a way that accurately captures the participants' main concerns and how they continually address those concerns. Last, the principle of modifiability dictates that the theory can never be more correct than its ability to work the data; thus, as the latter reveals itself in research, the former must constantly be modified.

As an example, I look at the various concepts that I presented in this book (e.g., the armory, minding the gap, disruptive innovation, etc.) and ask, "Do these categories fit the data? Are they relevant? Do they work the data?" The answer is yes, I believe they accurately reflect what emerged from the data. Like shame resilience theory, my quantitative colleagues will test my theories on Wholeheartedness and vulnerability and we will push the knowledge development process forward.

As I look back on this journey, I realize the deep truth in the quote I shared at the beginning of this chapter. There really is no path. Because the research participants had the courage to share their stories, experiences, and wisdom, I forged a path that defined my career and my life. When I first realized and resented the importance of embracing vulnerability and living a Wholehearted life, I would tell people that I was hijacked by my own data. Now, I know that I was rescued by it.

PRACTICING GRATITUDE

It is not joy that makes us grateful; it is gratitude that makes us joyful.

—Brother David Steindl-Rast

To my literary agents, Jo-Lynne Worley and Joanie Shoemaker: Thank you for believing in me and in the work.

To my manager, Murdoch Mackinnon: "You're a great copilot. Here's to landing more planes."

To my writing teacher and editor, Polly Koch: I literally couldn't do it without you. I'm so grateful.

To Jessica Sindler, my editor at Gotham: Thank you for your wisdom, insight, and the super-fun sleepover. I feel like I won the editor lottery.

To my publisher Bill Shinker and to the entire Gotham team, Monica Benalcazar, Spring Hoteling, Pete Garceau, Lisa Johnson, Anne Kosmoski, Casey Maloney, Lauren Marino, Sophia Muthuraj, Erica Ferguson, and Craig Schneider: Thank you for your talent, patience, and enthusiasm.

Gratitude to the gang at Speaker's Office: Holli Catch-pole, Jenny Canzoneri, Kristen Fine, Cassie Glasgow, Marsha Horshok, Michele Rubino, and Kim Stark: *Hey JCan! Am I supposed to be in Edmonton?*

So grateful for the talent and artistry of graphic designer Elan Morgan and for the amazing work of artist Nicholas Wilton. Thanks to Vincent Hyman for his editing talent and to Jayme Johnson of Worthy Marketing Group for her communication and connection wisdom.

Thank you to the friends who challenge me to show up, be brave, and dare greatly: Jimmy Bartz, Negash Berhanu, Shiferaw Berhanu, Farrah Braniff, Wendy Burks, Katherine Center, Tracey Clark, Ronda Dearing, Laura Easton, Kris Edelheit, Beverly and Chip Edens, Mike Erwin, Frieda Fromen, Peter Fuda, Ali Edwards, Margarita Flores, Jen Grey, Dawn Hedgepeth, Robert Hilliker, Karen Holmes, Andrea Corona Jenkins, Myriam Joseph, Charles Kiley, Jenny Lawson, Jen Lee, Jen Lemen, Harriet Lerner, Elizabeth Lesser, Susie Loredo, Laura Mayes, Mati Rose McDonough, Patrick Miller, Whitney Ogle, Joe Reynolds, Kelly Rae Roberts, Virginia Rondero-Hernandez, Gretchen Rubin, Andrea Scher, Peter Sheahan, Eileen Singleton, Diana Storms, Alessandra de Souza, Ria Unson, Karen Walrond, Jess Weiner, Maile Wilson, Eric Williams, and Laura Williams.

To the curators of TEDx Houston: Javier Fadul, Kara Matheny, and Tim DeSilva. Thank you for trusting me and taking a chance.

To the larger TED family: In 1998 I told Steve that my dream was to start a national conversation about shame. Thank you for making that dream come true. Thank you to Chris Anderson, Kelly Stoetzel, June Cohen, Tom Rielly,

Nicholas Weinberg, Mike Lundgren, and the entire team of idea spreaders and dream makers.

To my research assistants, Saba Khonsari and Yolanda Villarreal: Thank you for your commitment, patience, and hard work.

To our parents: Deanne Rogers and David Robinson, Molly May and Chuck Brown, Jacobina and Bill Alley, Corky and Jack Crisci: Thanks for always believing in us, loving us so fiercely, being totally crazy about our children, and teaching us to dare greatly.

To my sibs, Ashley and Amaya Ruiz; Barrett, Frankie, and Gabi Guillen; Jason Brown; and Jen and David Alley: Thank you for the love, support, laughter, tears, high fives, and fist bumps.

To Steve, Ellen, and Charlie: Y'all make everything possible. I don't know how I got so lucky. I love you.

NOTES AND REFERENCES

INTRODUCTION

p. 8   . . . developing a theory:

Brown, Brené. (2009). *Connections: A 12-session psychoeducational shame-resilience curriculum.* Center City, MN: Hazelden.

Brown, Brené. (2007). *I Thought It Was Just Me (But It Isn't): Telling the Truth About Perfectionism, Inadequacy, and Power.* New York: Penguin/Gotham Books.

Brown, Brené. (2007). Shame resilience theory. In Susan P. Robbins, Pranab Chatterjee, and Edward R. Canda (Eds.), *Contemporary human behavior theory: A critical perspective for social work*, rev. ed. Boston: Allyn and Bacon.

Brown, Brené. (2006). Shame resilience theory: A grounded theory study on women and shame. *Families in Society, 87,* 1: 43–52.

p. 9   *The Gifts of Imperfection*: Brown, B. (2010). *The gifts of imperfection: Letting go of who we think we should be and embracing who we are.* Center City, MN: Hazelden.

p. 12   . . . in my dissertation: Brown, C.B. (2002). Acompañar: A grounded theory of developing, maintaining and assessing relevance in professional helping. Dissertation Abstracts International, 63(02). (UMI No. 3041999).

p. 13   TEDxHouston

p. 14   ... the main TED website

p. 14   ... the main TED conference in Long Beach, CA.

CHAPTER 1
SCARCITY: LOOKING INSIDE OUR CULTURE OF "NEVER ENOUGH"

p. 20   Recently a group of researchers conducted a computer analysis: DeWall, C. Nathan; Pond Jr., Richard S.; Campbell, W. Keith; Twenge, J. (2011). Tuning in to psychological change: Linguistic markers of psychological traits and emotions over time in popular US song lyrics. *Psychology of Aesthetics, Creativity, and the Arts 5*, 3: 200–207.

p. 20   *The Narcissism Epidemic*: Twenge, J., and Campbell, K. (2009). *The narcissism epidemic: Living in the age of entitlement*. New York: Simon and Schuster.

p. 25   *The Soul of Money*: Twist, L. (2003). *The soul of money: Transforming your relationship with money and life* (New York: W. W. Norton and Company), p. 44.

p. 26   The word *scarce:* Merriam-Webster. Retrieved January 2012. http://www.merriam-webster.com/dictionary/

CHAPTER 2
DEBUNKING THE VULNERABILITY MYTHS

p. 39   From the field of health psychology: Aiken, L., Gerend, M., and Jackson, K. (2001). Subjective risk and health protective behavior: Cancer screening and cancer prevention. In A. Baum, T. Revenson, and J. Singer (Eds.), *Handbook of health psychology*, pp. 727–746. Mahwah, NJ: Erlbaum.

Apanovitch, A., Salovey, P., and Merson, M. (1998). The Yale-MTV study of attitudes of American youth. Manuscript in preparation.

p. 40   From the field of social psychology: Sagarin, B., Cialdini, R., Rice, W., and Serna, S. (2002). Dispelling the illusion of invulnerability: The motivations and mechanisms of resistance to persuasion. *Journal of Personality and Social Psychology, 83*, 3: 536–541.

p. 50 *The Science of Trust*: Gottman, J. (2011). *The science of trust: Emotional attunement for couples.* New York: W. W. Norton & Company.

p. 50 . . . the University of California–Berkeley's "Greater Good": John Gottman on Trust and Betrayal. October 28, 2011. Retrieved February 2012. http://greatergood.berkeley .edu/article/item/john_gottman_on_trust_and_betrayal/ (www.greatergood.berkeley.edu)

p. 54 There's actually some very persuasive leadership research: Fuda, P., and Badham, R. (2011). Fire, snowball, mask, movie: How leaders spark and sustain change. *Harvard Business Review. http://hbr.org/2011/11/fire-snowball-mask-movie-how-leaders-spark-and-sustain-change/ar/1*

CHAPTER 3
UNDERSTANDING AND COMBATING SHAME
(AKA GREMLIN NINJA WARRIOR TRAINING)

p. 71 In a 2011 study: Kross, E., Berman, M., Mischel, W., Smith, E. E., & Wager, T. (2011). Social rejection shares somatosensory representations with physical pain. *Proceedings of the National Academy of Sciences, 108*, 15: 6270–6275.

p. 71 The majority of shame researchers: For the most comprehensive review of the shame and guilt literature see *Shame and Guilt* by June Price Tangney and Ronda L. Dearing (New York: Guilford Press, 2002).

Additionally, I recommend this edited volume: *Shame in the Therapy Hour* edited by Ronda Dearing and June Tangney (American Psychological Association, 2011).

p. 73 Shame is highly correlated, and Researchers don't find . . . : The following books and articles explore the relationships between shame and various outcomes:

Balcom, D., Lee, R., and Tager, J. (1995). The systematic treatment of shame in couples. *Journal of Marital and Family Therapy, 21:* 55–65.

Brown, B. (2007). *I thought it was just me: Women reclaiming power in a culture of shame.* New York: Gotham.

Brown, B (2006). Shame resilience theory: A Grounded theory study on women and shame. *Families in Society, 87,* 1: 43–52.

Dearing, R., and Tangney, J. (Eds). (2011). *Shame in the therapy hour.* American Psychological Association.

Dearing, R., Stuewig, J., and Tangney, J. (2005). On the importance of distinguishing shame from guilt: Relations to problematic alcohol and drug use. *Addictive Behaviors, 30:* 1392–1404.

Ferguson, T. J., Eyre, H. L., and Ashbaker, M. (2000). Unwanted identities: A key variable in shame-anger links and gender differences in shame. *Sex Roles, 42:* 133–157.

Hartling, L., Rosen, W., Walker, M., and Jordan, J. (2000). *Shame and humiliation: From isolation to relational transformation* (Work in Progress No. 88). Wellesley, MA: The Stone Center, Wellesley College.

Jordan, J. (1989). *Relational development: Therapeutic implications of empathy and shame* (Work in Progress No. 39). Wellesley, MA: The Stone Center, Wellesley College.

Lester, D. (1997). The role of shame in suicide. *Suicide and Life-Threatening Behavior, 27:* 352–361.

Lewis, H. B. (1971). *Shame and guilt in neurosis.* New York: International Universities Press.

Mason, M. (1991). Women and shame: Kin and culture. In C. Bepko (ed.), *Feminism and addiction,* pp. 175–194. Binghamton, NY: Haworth.

Nathanson, D. (1997). Affect theory and the compass of shame. In M. Lansky and A. Morrison (Eds.), *The widening scope of shame.* Hillsdale, NJ: Analytic.

Sabatino, C. (1999). Men facing their vulnerabilities: Group processes for men who have sexually offended. *Journal of Men's Studies, 8:* 83–90.

Scheff, T. (2000). Shame and the social bond: A sociological theory. *Sociological Theory, 18:* 84–99.

Scheff, T. (2003). Shame in self and society. *Symbolic Interaction, 26:* 239–262.

Stuewig, J., Tangney, J. P., Mashek, D., Forkner, P., and Dearing, R. (2009). The moral emotions, alcohol dependence, and HIV risk behavior in an incarcerated sample. *Substance Use and Misuse, 44:* 449–471.

Talbot, N. (1995). Unearthing shame is the supervisory experience. *American Journal of Psychotherapy, 49:* 338–349.

Tangney, J. P., Stuewig, J., and Hafez, L. (in press). Shame, guilt and remorse: Implications for offender populations. *Journal of Forensic Psychiatry & Psychology.*

Tangney, J. P., Stuewig, J., Mashek, D., and Hastings, M. (2011). Assessing jail inmates' proneness to shame and guilt: Feeling bad about the behavior or the self? *Criminal Justice and Behavior, 38:* 710–734.

Tangney, J. P. (1992). Situational determinants of shame and guilt in young adulthood. *Personality and Social Psychology Bulletin, 18:* 199–206.

Tangney, J. P., and Dearing, R. (2002). *Shame and guilt.* New York: Guilford.

p. 73   Humiliation is another word: Klein, D. C. (1991). The humiliation dynamic. An overview. *The Journal of Primary Prevention, 12,* 2: 93–122.

p. 76   *Incognito*: Eagleman, D. (2011*). Incognito: The secret lives of the brain.* New York: Pantheon.

p. 77   Research from the Stone Center at Wellesley: Hartling, L., Rosen, W., Walker, M., and Jordan, J. (2000). Shame and humiliation: From isolation to relational transformation (*Work in Progress No. 88*). Wellesley, MA: The Stone Center, Wellesley College.

p. 82   James Pennebaker's work:
Pennebaker, J. W. (2004). *Writing to heal: A guided journal for recovering from trauma and emotional upheaval.* Oakland: New Harbinger Publications.

Pennebaker, J. W. (2010). Expressive writing in a clinical setting. *The Independent Practitioner, 30:* 23–25.

Petrie, K. J., Booth, R. J., and Pennebaker, J. W. (1998). The immunological effects of thought suppression. *Journal of Personality and Social Psychology, 75:* 1264–1272.

Pennebaker, J. W., Kiecolt-Glaser, J., and Glaser, R. (1988). Disclosure of traumas and immune function: Health implications for psychotherapy. *Journal of Consulting and Clinical Psychology, 56:* 239–245.

Richards, J. M., Beal, W. E., Seagal, J., and Pennebaker, J. W. (2000). The effects of disclosure of traumatic events on illness behavior among psychiatric prison inmates. *Journal of Abnormal Psychology, 109:* 156–160.

p. 82   Pennebaker, J. W. (2004). *Writing to heal: A guided journal for recovering from trauma and emotional upheaval.* Oakland: New Harbinger Publications.

p. 88   Marilyn Frye describes a double bind: Frye, M. (2001). Oppression. In M. Anderson and P. Collins (Eds.), *Race, class and gender: An anthology.* New York: Wadsworth.

p. 89   In a US study on conformity to feminine norms: Mahalik, J. R., Morray, E., Coonerty-Femiano, A., Ludlow, L. H., Slattery, S. M., and Smiler, A. (2005). Development of the conformity to feminine norms inventory. *Sex Roles, 52:* 317–335.

p. 99   What's ironic (or perhaps natural) is that research tells us that we judge people: Shrauger, S., and Patterson, M. (1974). Self-evaluation and the selection of dimensions for evaluating others. *Journal of Personality, 42,* 569–585.

p. 100   I wrote an op-ed on bullying: Brown, B. (September 30, 2002). Reality TV bites: Bracing for a new season of bullies [op-ed]. *Houston Chronicle,* p. 23A.

p. 107 Well, when looking at the attributes associated with masculinity in the US: Mahalik, J. R., Locke, B., Ludlow, L., Diemer, M., Scott, R. P. J., Gottfried, M., and Freitas, G. (2003). Development of the Conformity to Masculine Norms Inventory. *Psychology of Men and Masculinity, 4*: 3–25.

Brown, C. B. (2002). Acompañar: A grounded theory of developing, maintaining and assessing relevance in professional helping. *Dissertation Abstracts International, 63*(02). (UMI No. 3041999).

Brown, B. (2010). *The gifts of imperfection: Letting go of who we think we should be and embracing who we are.* Center City, MN: Hazelden.

Brown, B. (2010). Shame resilience theory. In S. P. Robbins, P. Chatterjee, and E. R. Canda (Eds.), *Contemporary human behavior theory: A critical perspective for social work,* rev. ed. Boston: Allyn and Bacon.

p. 110 *The Velveteen Rabbit*: Williams, Margery (1922). *The velveteen rabbit.* New York: Doubleday.

CHAPTER 4
THE VULNERABILITY ARMORY

p. 131 Dr. Kristen Neff:

Neff, K. (2011). *Self-compassion: Stop beating yourself up and leave insecurity behind.* New York: William Morrow.

Neff, K. (2003). Self-compassion: An alternative conceptualization of a healthy attitude toward oneself. *Self and Identity, 2*: 85–101.

Neff, K. (2003). The development and validation of a scale to measure self-compassion, *Self and Identity, 2*: 223–50.

p. 133 Gretchen Rubin: http://www.gretchenrubin.com/

Rubin, G. (2012). *Happier at home: Kiss more, jump more, abandon a project, read Samuel Johnson, and my other experi-*

ments in the practice of everyday life. New York: Crown Archetype.

Rubin, G. (2009). *The happiness project: Or, why I spent a year trying to sing in the morning, clean my closets, fight right, read Aristotle, and generally have more fun.* New York: Harper.

p. 133   Andrea Scher: http://www.superherojournal.com/ and http://www.superherophoto.com/

p. 135   Nicholas Wilton: http://nicholaswiltonpaintings.com/ and http://www.artplaneworkshop.com/

p. 137   Leonard Cohen: "Anthem," *The Future*, 1992, Columbia Records.

p. 138   The Centers for Disease Control:

Morbidity and Mortality Weekly Report (MMWR), November 2011: Vital Signs: Overdoses of Prescription Opioid Pain Relievers–United States, 1999–2008.

p. 138   Even more alarming: Stutman, Robert. 2011 lecture at The UP Experience. This video can be viewed here: http://www.thestutmangroup.com/media.html#video

p. 140   Jean Baker Miller and Irene Stiver: Miller, J. B., and Stiver, I. P. (1997). *The healing connection: How women form relationships in both therapy and in life.* Boston: Beacon Press.

p. 142   In Sir Ken Robinson's wonderful 2010 TED talk: http://www.ted.com/talks/lang/en/sir_ken_robinson_bring_on_the_revolution.html

p. 146   Jennifer Louden: http://jenniferlouden.com/

Louden, J. (2007). *The life organizer: A woman's guide to a mindful year.* Novato, CA: New World Library.

p. 147   The *Houston Chronicle*: Brown, B. (July 25, 2009). Time to get off the phone [op-ed]. *Houston Chronicle*, p. B7.

p. 152   My dissertation: Brown, C. B. (2002). Acompañar: A grounded theory of developing, maintaining and assessing relevance in professional helping. Dissertation Abstracts International, 63(02). (UMI No. 3041999).

p. 153   The statistics on post-traumatic-stress-related:

Parrish, K. (2011), Battaglia calls reducing suicides a top priority. American Forces Press Service. US Department of Defense. Harrell, M., and Berglass, N. (2011). Losing the battle: The challenge of military suicide. Center for New American Security Policy Brief.

p. 154   Craig Bryan, a University of Texas psychologist: Thompson, M. (April 13, 2010). *Is the army losing its war on suicide? Time* magazine.

p. 154   The American Bar Association: Weiss, D. C. (2009). Perfectionism, "psychic battering" among reasons for lawyer depression. *American Bar Association Journal.*

p. 156   Team Red, White and Blue: http://www.teamrwb.org/

p. 164   *The In-Laws: The In-Laws* (1979). Warner Bros. Pictures.

p. 171   *Almost Famous: Almost Famous* (2000). DreamWorks Studios.

p. 171   Scott Stratten: http://www.unmarketing.com/

Stratten, S. (2010). *Unmarketing: Stop marketing. Start engaging.* Hoboken: Wiley.

CHAPTER 5
MIND THE GAP: CULTIVATING CHANGE AND CLOSING THE DISENGAGEMENT DIVIDE

p. 174   Terrence Deal and Allan Kennedy: Deal, T. and Kennedy, A. (2000). *Corporate cultures. The rites and rituals of corporate life.* New York: Perseus.

CHAPTER 6
DISRUPTIVE ENGAGEMENT: DARING TO REHUMANIZE EDUCATION AND WORK

p. 188   Sir Ken Robinson speaks: Robinson, K. (2011). Second Edition. *Out of our minds: Learning to be creative.* Bloomington, MN: Capstone Publishing.

p. 190   The Workplace Bullying Institute: http://www.workplace bullying.org/wbiresearch/2010-wbi-national-survey/

p. 190   . . . bullied at work: Deschenaux, J. (2007). *Experts: Antibullying policies increase productivity.* Retrieved from http:// www.shrm.org/LegalIssues/EmploymentLaw

p. 194   Bill Gates wrote this in a *New York Times* op-ed: Gates, B. (February 22, 2012). Shame is not the solution [op-ed]. *The New York Times.*

p. 195   Shame researchers June Tangney and Ronda Dearing explain: Tangney, J. P., and Dearing, R. (2002). *Shame and guilt.* New York: Guilford.

p. 198   Writers like bell hooks and Paulo Freire:

Freire, P. (1970). *Pedagogy of the oppressed.* New York: Continuum.

hooks, b. (1994). *Teaching to transgress: Education as the price of freedom.* New York: Routledge.

p. 199   Dennis Saleebey: Saleebey, D. (1996). The strengths perspective in social work practice: Extensions and cautions. *Social Work, 41*, 3: 296–306.

p. 209   In a video interview with CNN/Money: http://manage ment.fortune.cnn.com/2012/03/16/lululemon-christine-day. Retrieved March 2012.

p. 211   Tribes: Godin, S. (2008). *Tribes: We need you to lead us.* New York: Portfolio.

CHAPTER 7
WHOLEHEARTED PARENTING: DARING TO BE THE ADULTS WE WANT OUR CHILDREN TO BE

p. 223   One of the very best pieces of parenting advice: *The Oprah Winfrey Show.* Harpo Studios. May 26, 2000.

p. 239   C. R. Snyder's research on hope:

Snyder, C. R. (2003). *Psychology of hope: You can get there from here,* paperback ed. New York: Free Press.

Snyder, C R., Lehman, Kenneth A., Kluck, Ben, and Monsson, Yngve. (2006). Hope for rehabilitation and vice versa." *Rehabilitation Psychology*, *51*, 2: 89–112.

Snyder, C. R. (2002). Hope theory: Rainbows in the mind." *Psychological Inquiry*, *13*, 4: 249–75.

APPENDIX
TRUST IN EMERGENCE: GROUNDED THEORY AND MY RESEARCH PROCESS

p. 252   Letting go of your own interests: Glaser, B., and Strauss, A. (1967). *The discovery of grounded theory.* Chicago: Aldine.

Glaser, B. (1978). *Theoretical sensitivity: Advances in the methodology of grounded theory.* Mill Valley, CA: Sociological Press.

Glaser, B. (1992). *Basics of grounded theory: Emergence versus forming.* Mill Valley, CA: Sociological Press.

Glaser, B. (1998). *Doing grounded theory: Issues and discussions.* Mill Valley, CA: Sociological Press.

Glaser, B. (2001). *The grounded theory perspective: Conceptualization contrasted with description.* Mill Valley, CA: Sociological Press.

p. 252   Behavioral researcher Fred Kerlinger defines theory: Kerlinger, Fred N. (1973). *Foundations of behavioral research.* 2nd edition. New York: Holt, Rinehart and Winston.

p. 253   After developing a theory on shame resilience: Brown, 2004, 2005, 2009, 2010.

p. 255   Originally developed by Glaser and Strauss: Glaser, B., and Strauss, A. (1967). *The discovery of grounded theory.* Chicago: Aldine.

p. 255   Refined by Glaser: Glaser, 1978, 1992, 1998, 2001.

p. 255   When using theoretical sampling: Glaser, 1978.

p. 255   One important tenet of grounded theory: Glaser, 1978, 1998, 2001.

p. 256 A basic tenet of grounded theory is "all is data": Glaser, 1998.

p. 257 Adjusted conversational interviewing: Glaser, 1978, 1998.

p. 258 Grounded theory researchers are required: Glaser, 1978, 1998, 2001.

p. 258 . . . theory is generated from the data: Glaser, 1978, 1998, 2001.

p. 259 According to Glaser: Glaser, 1998.

p. 259 . . . keeping an existing theory intact: Glaser, 1998.

p. 259 . . . allow the core problems and processes to emerge: Glaser, 1992; Glaser, 1998.

p. 259 Work the core of what is going on: Glaser, 1998.

p. 260 . . . the former must be constantly modified: Glaser, 1978.

INDEX

ABOUT THE AUTHOR

Brené Brown, Ph.D., LMSW is a research professor at the University of Houston Graduate College of Social Work. She is a nationally renowned speaker and has won numerous teaching awards, including the College's Outstanding Faculty Award. Her groundbreaking research has been featured on PBS, NPR, and CNN. Brené's 2010 TEDxHouston talk, *The Power of Vulnerability*, is one of the top ten most viewed TED talks on TED.com, with approximately 5 million viewers. Additionally, Brené gave the closing talk at the 2012 TED conference, where she talked about shame, courage, and innovation. She is also the author of *The Gifts of Imperfection* (2010), *I Thought It Was Just Me* (2007), and *Connections* (2009), a shame-resilience curriculum being facilitated by helping professionals around the world. Brené lives in Houston with her husband, Steve, and their two children, Ellen and Charlie.